THE AUDIT REPORT

What it says and what it means

J. C. Shaw, BL, CA, FCMA, JDipMA
Partner in Deloitte Haskins & Sells, Edinburgh
Johnstone Smith Professor of Accountancy,
University of Glasgow

Published for
THE INSTITUTE OF CHARTERED
ACCOUNTANTS OF SCOTLAND
by
GEE & CO (PUBLISHERS) LIMITED
151 STRAND, LONDON WC2R 1JJ

FIRST PUBLISHED 1980
GEE & CO (PUBLISHERS) LIMITED

ISBN 0 85258 203X

This monograph, the first in a series of five, is published for the Research Advisory Committee of The Institute of Chartered Accountants of Scotland and does not necessarily represent the views either of the Research Advisory Committee or of the Council of the Institute.

No responsibility for loss occasioned to any person acting or refraining from action as a result of any material in this publication can be accepted by the authors or publisher.

Printed in Great Britain for Gee & Co (Publishers) Limited
by Cheney & Sons Ltd., Banbury, Oxon.

Foreword

This series of monographs has been initiated by the Research Advisory Committee of The Institute of Chartered Accountants of Scotland. The Committee believes that, at a time both of change and of increasing interest in accounting information, these monographs will meet a need for clear explanation of some of the more difficult concepts relevant to the preparation of corporate accounting reports. All are written by acknowledged experts in their respective fields in a style which will appeal equally to the specialist and the well informed general reader. Some will be relevant to the needs of one group more than to another, but they are addressed principally to accountants, bankers, civil servants, directors, financial journalists, investment managers, investment analysts, private investors, managers, trade union officials and others with an interest in accounting information. Opinions expressed by the authors are, of course, their own.

David Flint,
Convener, Research Advisory Committee,
The Institute of Chartered Accountants of Scotland,
Edinburgh.

September 1980.

Contents

Preface

The audit report is an important element both in the exercise of control within the individual company and in the process of social control of the corporate sector of the economy. The discussion which follows is addressed neither to the specialist nor to the man in the street; it is neither an auditing treatise nor a "plain man's guide to the audit report". Accountancy or auditing specialists may well find the brief overview to be superficial, but it is hoped that the commentary will help the interested "non-specialist" user of financial statements. The reader is assumed to be already familiar with general concepts of financial measurement and financial reporting and to be able to review the financial statements of an individual company with reasonable confidence in his ability to interpret them properly. The explanation which follows, of the meaning of the audit report and of the audit process on which the report is based, is intended to provide a deeper understanding of the nature of audit objectives and of the nature and extent of assurance which can be drawn from the unqualified audit opinion.

The paper is presented in two parts. Part I provides an explanation of what the words of the audit report mean. It seeks to explain what the reader should understand from the terms of the audit report and refers to its implied terms as well as to the explicit wording. Part II provides a brief explanation of the main characteristics of the audit function and process and is intended to provide a clearer understanding of the basis for interpreting the audit report itself. Although Part I has been written as a substantially self-contained exposition, Part II is integral to a fuller understanding of the discussion.

The law requires the annual accounts of every limited company to be audited and reported on by the auditor.[1] The audit report thus becomes part of the company's annual report. Audited accounts determine the legality of

[1] Companies Act 1948, S. 156(1).

certain transactions including questions of dividend distribution.[2] The audit report is actually read aloud at the annual general meeting of the company to which the accounts are submitted. Despite the frequency with which it appears and despite its importance, however, the audit report is neither well nor widely understood. Although it conventionally consists of a few, highly formalised sentences, totalling about 100 words, the audit report is based on rigorous work by experienced and highly trained professionals. This work often extends over many man-weeks and involves significant cost in the form of audit fees (which have to be specifically disclosed in the annual accounts).

Developments in the theory and practice of accounting respond to changes in the perceived priorities of society – or of sectional interests in society. Auditing, which is to do with accounting and accountability, is equally socially responsive. The present "state of the art" as described here will certainly change. Examples of change can be found in the rapidly developing appreciation of the validity of conflicting claims and interests of different "stakeholders"* in the corporate enterprise. Recognition of these conflicting claims coincides with greater awareness of the community of interest among all "stakeholders" in the economic survival and success of the business enterprise; for example, explicit directors' responsibilities towards employees[3] as well as to shareholders. The present conventional view of the audit role will similarly be modified and developed in response to inevitable social change.

The auditing profession's responses to changing social perceptions of accountability and to changing views of the information needs of users of accounts stimulate technical changes in the process and discharge of the auditing function. Such developments can be illustrated by the discussion about the terms in which the auditor should report on CCA (current cost accounting) financial statements. Another example can be found in the suggestions that so-called "small companies" might be relieved from some detailed requirements of financial disclosure and/or from the requirement for compulsory audit. Although discussion about these and other future developments lies beyond the scope of this paper, brief reference is made in Section 9 to some unresolved problems.

There is no discussion here of the many organisations and enterprises which are not constituted as companies limited by share capital but whose

* By "stakeholder" is meant individual interests associated with the entity and dependent upon it – shareholders, employees, suppliers, customers, lenders and management.

[2] Companies Act 1980, S. 43(3).

[3] Companies Act 1980, S. 46.

financial reports include an audit report – for example, local authorities, universities, charities, nationalised industries. The discussion is restricted to the audit report on the financial statements of a limited company. The discussion is further restricted in that it relates to the audit report which confirms that all is well – that is, the unqualified audit opinion.

Statistics indicate that there are approximately 735,000 limited companies registered in the United Kingdom. Even if one excludes the large number of dormant or inactive companies (which still have to submit accounts to audit), there are some hundreds of thousands of active companies. Each one of these is required by law to prepare and make public an annual report which includes financial statements;[4] the principal financial statements comprise the audited accounts – profit and loss account, balance sheet, statement of source and use of funds and notes. Publication of the annual report involves the issue of a copy to every registered shareholder of the company and the lodging with the Registrar of Companies of a copy available for public inspection. Some companies – mainly, but not exclusively, those whose shares are listed on the Stock Exchange – publicise their financial results even more extensively by paid newspaper advertisements and extensive circulation of extracts from their annual report.

This monograph was commissioned by the Research Advisory Committee of The Institute of Chartered Accountants of Scotland, which appointed a small technical advisory committee consisting of Professor David Flint (University of Glasgow and a former President of ICAS), Ian MacLeod (Financial Director, Parsons Peebles Ltd), Peter N. McMonnies (UK Director of Accounting and Auditing Research, Thomson McLintock & Co) and Professor David Tweedie (Technical Director, ICAS). My debt to them is immense, they read patiently and commented wisely on early drafts and provided invaluable advice and encouragement, without which this paper would still be a project. I received similarly helpful advice and comment from practising colleagues in Deloitte Haskins & Sells, from academic colleagues in the Department of Accountancy at the University of Glasgow and from other professional colleagues of The Institute of Chartered Accountants of Scotland. To those and many others who have helped in various ways I express, inadequately, my grateful thanks. Three people in particular deserve special mention: Mrs. Peggy Jackson, who provided detailed references, read proofs and nursed early drafts through various stages of detailed editing; Mrs. Eleanor McIntosh, who typed so expertly the many versions of the manuscript (not always easily legible in its original form!); and Miss Win Elliott (Editor of

[4] Companies Act 1976, S. 1.

The Accountant's Magazine), who prepared the draft for publication and completed detailed final editing.

In spite of such wide-ranging help and encouragement, the responsibility for opinions expressed remains mine alone. The views expressed must not be taken in any way as representing those of The Institute of Chartered Accountants of Scotland nor of Deloitte Haskins & Sells. However, I hope that they would be prepared at least to discuss them. Despite these important disclaimers, I hope that I have managed to provide a true and fair view of what the audit report means!

J. C. Shaw
June 1980.

PART I

1 *Introduction to Accounting*

Accountability

The preface indicates that this paper is intended for the reader who is an informed layman – someone who is not a specialist but who is not completely lost in the world of financial reporting. Despite the assumption of the reader's basic awareness of the nature and process of accounting, it may be helpful to review these processes very briefly. Such a review will ensure that discussion of the audit report proceeds from common ground. It will also serve to emphasise the distinguishable responsibilities of the directors as compared with those of the auditor and will highlight the nature of the problems which directors confront in discharging their responsibilities. The second section, which follows, provides a parallel introduction to auditing. Taken together these two introductions should put into context the detailed exploration of the audit report.

United Kingdom legal requirements give expression to two slightly different perceptions of the duty of accountability. The more obvious is the "stewardship" (or "trustee" or "agency") concept under which members of the board of directors are seen to act as the custodians and guardians of resources entrusted to them by shareholders, who elect them to the board. (The resources take the form of subscribed capital and retained surpluses). As "stewards", the directors individually and the board collectively owe a duty to account to shareholders so that they can be informed of the actions of the directors. Shareholders can use the reported information to form a view of the effectiveness with which the directors are using the resources entrusted to their management. A second, wider, concept discerns that those who seek to allocate resources and to take decisions owe a duty to account to all those who can claim an interest either in the resources being allocated or in the decisions being taken. It is argued that in the context of the modern company various separate interests ("stakeholders") co-operate in the creation of wealth – shareholders, lenders, employees, suppliers, customers, the State and the local community – and that the board effectively acts as the arbiter of the allocation among them of the results of the enterprise. Board decisions in this role demand scrutiny from each interest group; each group can be expected to seek assurance that the total wealth created has been allocated or attributed "fairly" among the competing claimants.

The obligation imposed by law on directors to prepare and publish a financial report, therefore, both derives from and expresses wide-ranging concepts of accountability. An initially restricted view of a duty of accountability by directors (who manage resources) to shareholders (who provide resources) has been progressively and considerably extended in response to social changes. The limited company, long recognised as a *legal* entity, is now recognised as an important *social* entity. It is seen as a powerful economic and social influence in the society (or societies) within which it operates. The activities of the limited company have implications for shareholders, for lenders, for employees, for suppliers, for customers and for the community at large. All these sectional interests are affected to a greater or lesser extent by the company's actions in creating wealth and in allocating the results of economic activity. Not least, all members of society are affected by the impact of the company's activity on the physical environment. Those who direct and manage the activities of the company, who are responsible for decisions which affect all the sectional interests in the company, and on whom depend decisions which result in the creation and allocation of wealth – that is, the directors – bear a heavy responsibility of accountability. Their duty is discharged in part by the preparation and publication of financial statements.

Statute law further imposes on directors of limited companies explicit and specific responsibilities with regard to:

(a) the maintenance of accounting records,[1] and

(b) the preparation of financial statements.[2]

The objectives of these requirements can be summarised as being to ensure:

[1] Companies Act 1976, S. 12.
[2] Companies Act 1976, S. 1.

(i) that proper control is exercised over all the resources entrusted to management; and

(ii) that proper accounting is made so that others may judge the effectiveness with which management has deployed these resources (and the "fairness" with which benefits have been allocated).

Perhaps the most demanding statutory obligation imposed on directors is to prepare and publish accounts which show a "true and fair view" of the results of the company during a period (usually a year) and of its state of affairs at the end of that period.[3]

What constitutes a "true and fair view" is not defined; perhaps, as with an elephant, you recognise it when you see it! The concept of true and fair is concerned more with understanding the "spirit" than with complying with the "letter" of the law. It is probably easier to identify and define what constitutes unacceptable financial reporting than it is to define how to achieve a "true and fair view", but it does not follow that any process of financial measurement and/or disclosure which cannot be identified as "unacceptable" will therefore necessarily be consistent with the disclosure of a "true and fair view". (An American phrase, "substance over form", is often interpreted as being analogous to "true and fair" – or at least comprehended by it. "Substance over form" implies that accounts will depict the economic reality of business events and transactions and not just their legalistic, apparent form). It has been suggested that "true and fair" is equivalent to "full and frank" and implies the absence of bias. That requires that the accounts as presented will not pre-condition a user's perception of the economic reality which they purport to represent. The accounts should not confuse or bias the conclusions which the user reaches in judging the effectiveness and fairness with which the board has used and allocated resources. But not only must the accounts have the virtue of being *unbiased*, they must contain information which is *adequate* for the purposes of the user. There are many obvious problems associated with attaining these objectives, not least the difficulty of identifying "users" and "user needs".

Accounts which give a true and fair view, however, do not result entirely from individually-determined systems and methods of financial measurement. Over many centuries certain conventions have evolved which now constrain the practical processes of accounting. The conventions of accounting become particularly relevant in the context of directors' obligations to maintain accounting records. These conventions condition the per-

[3] Companies Act 1948, S. 149(1).

ception of which items should be recognised as assets or as liabilities, which as expenditure or as income; how assets, liabilities and net income should be measured; how financial information should be summarised and how analysed for publication.

Accounting Conventions

The maintenance of accounting records demands consideration of techniques and procedures of financial measurement. The process of financial measurement involves the transformation into numerical form of events and relationships in the business world. Financial measurements, however, differ from other common types of measurement in that they are not derived from, and cannot be related to, objectively determined physical constants – as, for example, heat, speed, length, noise, etc. can be. Some conventional financial measurements can be objectively determined at the point of cash exchange or transfer – for example the cash cost of equipment bought, the cost of raw materials procured and of wages paid, even the listed catalogue price of goods sold. However, most of the important financial measurements depend upon subjective judgment: how long will the equipment operate and how much of its total cost should be set against the income derived from its use during only part of its total useful life? What figure should be attributed to goods manufactured during one period but unsold at the end of it? How should partially completed products be dealt with? How confident can the seller be that his customer will pay in full and not default?

These simple illustrations exemplify two of the basic precepts of accounting practice – the "matching" and the "prudence" concepts. By "matching" is meant the allocation of the financial effect of transactions into appropriate time periods so that relevant income and expenditure is matched. It avoids, at the extreme, reporting all outlays in one period and all income in another. "Prudence" is to some extent in conflict with "matching": application of the precept of prudence will involve deliberate mismatching of expenditure and possible income. In its crudest form, "prudence" means reporting a cautious view. Put simply, prudence recognises loss when its incidence appears likely but delays recognition of profit until realisation is virtually assured. Prudence also involves careful assessment of the need for, and the creation of, provisions against potential or likely loss. It also conditions the perception of which items should be recognised as assets in the balance sheet and which should be written off against profits as expenditure is incurred. Obviously, the practical application of these two precepts involves subjective judgment.

The determination of appropriate detailed accounting policies to be applied within these precepts also involves the careful exercise of skilled judgment. Because accounting seeks to portray business reality in neutral terms, the accounting policies adopted will inevitably reflect the managerial perceptions of what that reality is. (See Section 2 for some further discussion). It is therefore unlikely that the law, or any other regulatory agency, can specify techniques of financial measurement as "standard" in any sense that is analogous to existing standards of physical measurement. (To a very limited extent the EEC 4th Directive – adopted by the Council of Ministers in July 1978 – the requirements of which will in due course be enacted in UK law, prescribes specific measurement procedures. For example, expenditure incurred in the acquisition of the goodwill of a business, or attributed to such acquisition, is to be written off against profits over a maximum period of time.[4] A further example is that, whatever other information may be provided, the "normal" basis of accounting will be historical cost.[5] Such limited examples may be referred to as illustrations of the need to rely on legal enactment in order to achieve universally applicable "standards").

The preparation of financial statements demands consideration of detailed procedures of financial disclosure. As explained above, judgment is inevitably involved in nearly every aspect of the selection and application of policies and practices of financial measurement. Similarly, financial disclosure demands the exercise of judgment to ensure that the *manner* of presentation of the financial data does not distort the lack of bias striven for in the selection of measurement methods. The balance between summarisation and expansion of detail exemplifies the problems of disclosure – excessive summarisation, condensation or simplification may obscure important detailed information, but, conversely, excessive detail may unbalance the presentation, distort the general impression, and by "information overload" overwhelm the user's capacity to comprehend the information being disclosed.

With disclosure, at least, both the law and regulatory agencies can provide some assistance by identifying *minimum* specific disclosure *requirements.*[6] Such requirements are broadly of two types:

(i) information which is necessary (but not of itself sufficient) for a true and fair view – *eg*, details of purchases, disposals, and depreciation of different types of fixed asset;

[4] EEC 4th Directive, article 37(2).
[5] EEC 4th Directive, article 32.
[6] Companies Act 1967, Second Schedule and also Stock Exchange Listing Agreement, para. 9.

(ii) information which may not be directly relevant to a true and fair view but which is consistent with the duty of accountability to shareholders – *eg*, details of the remuneration of directors and of company funds applied for charitable or political purposes.

(It is sometimes suggested that there is a third type of information, one which is relevant to the wider duty of accountability beyond reporting to shareholders – *eg* numbers of employees and their aggregate wages). The over-riding requirement of the audited accounts is that, taken together, they should show a true and fair view; that is, they must go beyond merely satisfying the detailed requirements. (The provisions of the EEC 4th Directive will have to be considered in this context too, because when enacted in UK law they will require the adoption of a more rigidly specified format for financial statements than has hitherto been common in the UK. The over-riding objective of a "true and fair view" will, however, be preserved).

The financial statements which the law requires to be audited are the Profit and Loss Account and the Balance Sheet, together with related Notes.[7] (The EEC 4th Directive also deals only with these statements). In Britain, the accountancy profession has added to these legally specified requirements a Statement of Source and Application of Funds.[8] The inter-related financial statements comprised by Profit and Loss Account, Balance Sheet, Funds Statement and Notes thereto are referred to in this paper as "the accounts" or "the audited accounts". The audited accounts, however, comprise only part of the company's annual report. Audited accounts are published in conjunction with, at least, a Report by the Directors (required by law)[9] and frequently with extensive additional information such as a "Corporate Review", a separate "Statement by the Chairman" and supplementary statistical information. All of these other reports and statements will contain financial information and statements, often extensive, as part of the total communication between the company and the community, between the directors and the shareholders. As will be referred to in Section 3, the auditor will have regard to and will review all the figures in any document in which the audited accounts appear, but his explicit, direct, and inescapable responsibility and opinion relates only to the audited accounts as defined above – Profit and Loss Account, Balance Sheet, Statement of Source and Application of Funds and Notes to these Financial Statements.

[7] Companies Act 1948, S. 156(1).
[8] SSAP No. 10.
[9] Companies Act 1948, S. 157.

2 *Introduction to Auditing*

Following the introduction to concepts of accountability and to the nature of accounting conventions a similar introduction to auditing is required. This section will provide a very limited review of the nature of audit objectives. It will attempt to illustrate that the constraints imposed by conceptual and technical limitations to the process of accounting on the discharge by the directors of their responsibilities with regard to accountability are mirrored by constraints on the discharge by auditors of their reporting obligations imposed by conceptual and technical limitations to the process of auditing. A general understanding of these issues is essential to a proper understanding of the meaning of the audit report, which is to be discussed in detail in the next section. (The reader who wishes to extend his general understanding of auditing issues beyond that which it is hoped he will find here may find the later sections in Part II of interest, as they seek to provide more detailed discussion of auditing issues).

Audit Objectives

The professional societies which regulate the professional conduct of auditors (see Section 5) issued in April 1980 initial statements of Auditing Standards and Guidelines, which will be referred to again later at greater length. The Explanatory foreword (para. 2) to those statements defines an audit as follows:

> "An audit is the independent examination of, and expression of opinion on, the financial statements of an enterprise by an appointed auditor in pursuance of that appointment and in compliance with any relevant statutory obligation. The responsibility for the preparation of the financial statements and the presentation of the information included therein rests with the management of the enterprise (in the case of a

company, the directors). The auditor's responsibility is to report on the financial statements as presented by management."

Audit is to do with accountability, and the audit report expresses an opinion on accounts. The objective of the audit function can be summarised as being to confirm that the accounts prepared by the directors present a true and fair view. The audit opinion lends credibility to the directors' financial reporting by validating the techniques of financial measurement and reporting adopted by them. The audit opinion confirming the existence of a true and fair view implies affirmation of the absence of material error which, if present, would distort the user's perception of the economic reality portrayed by the accounts. Added credibility means greater usefulness for the accounts; therefore the explanation of audit objectives inevitably involves some reference to the objectives of the accounts themselves.

Essential features of financial reporting require that techniques of measurement and disclosure must be unbiased. The purpose of the financial report is to assist those who receive it to take informed decisions – including, for example, decisions about managerial effectiveness, or about the allocation of resources or about the "fairness" of dividends, wages, taxes or prices. The accounts themselves, therefore, should avoid providing bias to these decisions. If information is selected or presented in a way specifically intended to encourage some chosen effect on human behaviour it cannot be unbiased. If it is not unbiased it is not "reliable" from the point of view of those who wish to use the information to arrive at independent judgment. Independent judgments are best based on independent information – that is, on information obtained from a source independent of the activity or function being judged.

In the context of financial reporting the directors have the difficult task of providing the very information which is used as the basis for assessing their performance; those who are to be judged provide the evidence. The directors' direct interest in the results of the use of the accounts, therefore, may appear to conflict with their attainment of the objective of preparing accounts which are unbiased, which provide a true and fair view. This poses a problem of credibility and there follows a need for validation; users of accounts need confirmation that they do indeed present a true and fair view. Validation and confirmation of lack of bias are best provided independently of the source of the information.

Independent validation is provided by the auditor's independent, professional, opinion that the directors have succeeded in providing a "true and fair" view. It is important to emphasise that the auditor is independent of the directors; he is not part of the management. Furthermore, although formally appointed by them, the auditor is also independent of shareholders; he is not the "representative" or "agent" of any sectional interest group, and from his independent stance is well able to consider and detect any bias in the accounting presentation. (The issue of auditor independence, which is fundamental to the audit function, is touched on in a later section.)

The directors are responsible for determining the company's accounting policies, for selecting the financial measurement techniques they believe to be appropriate and for preparing financial statements which they believe will convey a true and fair view. (In practice the directors delegate much detailed work to appropriately qualified officials and executives, who together with the Board constitute "the management", but the *responsibility* remains collectively that of the directors). The audit report expresses an independent opinion as to their success in achieving disclosure of a true and fair view.

The auditor does not determine the policies or the techniques of measurement and disclosure. He may, however, contribute to the directors' efforts to give a true and fair view by helping them towards appropriate decisions. If the auditor were to conclude that the accounts prepared by management did not disclose a true and fair view – because of either measurement or disclosure deficiencies – he would make his adverse opinion clear to the management before publication. (There is less value to users in accounts which fail to show a true and fair view than in those that succeed in doing so). In such circumstances the management may well review its previous decisions and may alter its originally proposed policies and techniques so that the accounts accord with what the auditor could conclude would result in a true and fair view being given. There is, however, no formal obligation on the auditor to specify those policies or techniques which he thinks are appropriate.

The audit opinion does not say that the accounts are "correct"; it does not imply absolute accuracy; it does not imply that the financial policies and techniques are, in the opinion of the auditors, the only ones or the "best" ones. It certainly does not imply that the policies are the "best" in any absolute or objective sense. Since accuracy or "correctness" are inherently unattainable by the techniques and processes of financial measurement and reporting, there can be no "truest and fairest" view in any absolute sense. There may be "truer and fairer" views – indeed such possibilities are probably implied in the idea that there may be many perceptions of true and fair. The reporting obligations of directors are to present *a* true and fair view and that is what the unqualified audit opinion confirms has been achieved. The audit opinion is not concerned with comparatives any more than with absolutes. The auditor has to consider only if *a* true and fair view is represented; if so, an unqualified opinion is given; if not, then some form of qualification will be added. Changes in accounting methods and policies and in disclosure should result in an enhancement of the quality of the financial representation achieved; that is, in a truer and fairer view. Changes which do not tend in this direction are not improvements and should not be pursued. The unqualified audit opinion confirms that the financial statements convey a true and fair view – as that phrase is understood and within inescapable limits of materiality (to which further reference is made below).

Changes of accounting policy within the same company from year to year will usually result in the accounts for each year being properly judged by the auditor as giving a true and fair view at the relevant time. The changed accounting policy should recognise changed circumstances either of the reporting company or of the nature of its transactions or of the environment in which it is reporting. Changes in social or professional perceptions of how a true and fair view can be most effectively conveyed will also be reflected in changes of accounting policy. There is no implication in such changes that the more recent year's policies now give a true and fair view, which the previous year's failed to. The opinion that a true and fair view has been achieved in each year confirms that the financial statements reflect a reasonable representation of economic reality according to the circumstances of the time.

True and Fair

The phrase "true and fair" has become a term of art. It is not defined in the statute in which it appears (Companies Act 1948) nor by subsequent judicial process. Implications of the phrase "true and fair" include "valid", "impartial", "appropriate", "adequate", "relevant", "revealing". Accounts which are true and fair should portray the substantive effect of transactions and not simply their apparent form; they should portray an accurate representation of economic reality. As touched on in the previous paragraph, a "true and fair" view depends upon subjective criteria, and perceptions will change with circumstances. Because there are conceptual difficulties in defining the objectives of financial reporting, and because different representations of reality may be appropriate in different circumstances (or for different purposes), practical discussion of the concept of "true and fair" has to be related to specific circumstances. One might suggest that "true" relates to the degree of relative accuracy within any particular framework of economic/financial measurement and "fair" relates to the degree of completeness of the information in the form and context in which it is presented. "Fair" representation, on the other hand, may relate to the standard of judgment exercised by those who have to exercise subjective judgment in arriving at what they believe to be a "true" measurement or representation of economic events.

Materiality

Concepts of materiality relate to the purpose to which information is put. Limits to "materiality" in financial statements can perhaps be explained as very roughly analogous to engineering tolerances. Errors within the limits of engineering tolerances should not make a component useless; while not "perfect" it should still perform its function (if it fails, then the limit of tolerance has been wrongly specified). By analogy, errors or mis-statements in accounts which are not material should not invalidate the accounts for their intended use. On the other hand, the existence of material error is inconsistent with the representation of a true and fair view. Materiality in this context may relate either to financial measurement or to financial disclosure. The test of materiality remains that of impact on perception – would disclosure (or non-disclosure) or a different manner of disclosure change fundamentally the perception of the reader? If the answer is "yes" then an issue of materiality is involved. At this point the inter-relationship of the concepts of materiality and of true and fair should become clear.

Obviously, in considering his opinion about the true and fair view the auditor is much concerned with issues of materiality – of both measurement and disclosure. Concepts of materiality are inevitably subjective and depend upon the scale and nature of the business unit, the perceptions of management and the perceptions of the users of accounts. It is difficult to personify or even to identify clearly who the users of accounts are. Because their subjective perceptions reflect their individual objectives, it is probably impossible to discern general principles for defining limits to materiality. Each user of accounts expects that *material* items have been examined and that audited accounts do not contain *material* undetected errors. One of the auditor's many difficulties is in discerning the limits to users' perceptions of materiality. Ultimately, the auditor is forced to adopt his own criteria for establishing limits to materiality when considering and arriving at his audit opinion.

"Audit Risk"

The discussion of materiality can now be extended and related specifically to the audit opinion. Two aspects of the criteria referred to by the auditor in considering the validity of accounts are his perceptions of "materiality" and of "confidence". Both have to do with the possibility that undetected error will still exist after completion of the audit; that is, the "audit risk" expresses the degree of risk that audited accounts contain material undetected error. Management, in preparing accounts, has to confront the risk that they may contain material error not detected by the managerially imposed systems of control. Such controls include those on the security of custody of resources and controls on the application of the resources of the company, and also include (different) controls on the accuracy and integrity of the accounting systems. The "audit risk" is the risk that material errors undetected by management will still remain undetected at the end of the audit. The more narrowly we define the limits to the specification of materiality the less certain, or confident, we can be that all material errors have been detected; we can have a "high degree" of confidence that "large" errors have been detected, but a lower degree of confidence that "small" errors have been.

Going Concern

The auditor is not concerned to consider or express an opinion on the quality of the management – other than indirectly as inferred from his acceptance of their control procedures. If the audited accounts do provide an appropriate representation of economic reality, then users should be able to form their own judgment about managerial effectiveness. One limited instance in which the auditor has to consider specifically the effectiveness of management is in regard to its success in ensuring the continued short-term future existence of the enterprise. The "going concern" assumption is a fundamental concept of annual financial reporting.[1] This means that it is assumed that the business will continue in existence and there will be no dramatic change in its economic circumstances; it excludes the possibility of short-term break-up, forced sale or liquidation. Figures based on the going concern assumption are not related to realisation values (other than to a very limited extent in special circumstances). To the extent to which the going concern assumption is fundamental to the form and content of the accounts, therefore, the auditor indicates by inference his belief that it is the appropriate basis. He does not "guarantee" that the business *is* a going concern in

[1] SSAP No. 2, Statement of Accounting Policies.

the long term, but he does confirm that the assumption that it is a going concern is a valid basis for the financial statements.

3 *What the Audit Report Says*

Introduction

It was explained in the Preface that the range of this discussion is limited to the unqualified audit report on the accounts of limited companies based in the United Kingdom. Within even that restricted scope more than one form of audit report has to be considered. The wording of the audit report on the accounts of a company which has a subsidiary or subsidiaries (the parent company of a group) is different in some significant respects from the report on a limited company which does not have subsidiaries (a "single entity"). The detailed wording commonly used in audit reports current at the date of writing this monograph differs in some respects from the "standard" wording illustrated in the recently-published Auditing Standard on The Audit Report.[1] Because that Standard becomes effective for the audit of financial statements relating to accounting periods which *begin* on or after 1st April 1980, it is likely that the conventional wording currently in use will continue to be widely used until mid-1981. The discussion of the terms of the audit report therefore follows the sequence:–

(A) the audit report on the single entity;

(B) the audit report on the consolidated accounts of a parent company and group;

(C) the audit report illustrated in the Auditing Standard.[1]

Only the explicit terms of the report are discussed in this section. The implications of the audit report are dealt with in the next section.

[1] Auditing Standards and Guidelines: Auditing Standard – The Audit Report. The Institute of Chartered Accountants of Scotland (in conjunction with other accountancy bodies) 1980 – see Appendix I.

Illustrative examples of the wording of "typical" audit reports are given as a basis for discussion. Although the audit report is substantially standardised in format and has to deal specifically with certain statutorily-defined matters, the user of audited accounts will find that the detailed wording of an unqualified audit report varies from case to case, or at least from auditor to auditor (obviously the wording of a qualified audit report, by definition, varies from the "norm"). These differences, which will be detected in practice, serve to emphasise that the audit report is a personal statement of professional opinion, and the auditor will properly decide for himself the wording in which he chooses to express his opinion, constrained by a need to deal explicitly with certain statutorily-defined matters.

The two illustrations provided in the text are actual examples taken from audited accounts. There are some differences in wording which are not significant – for example, some audit reports refer to "profit" (or "loss") of the company, others less precisely to "the results"; some to accounts "for the year", others to accounts "for the period"; some refer to "acounts" others to "financial statements". Apparent anomalies of this kind have been left in the quoted examples. It is hoped that by the time he comes to the end of this section the reader will be able to identify insignificant variations in wording but to distinguish and understand the important significant differences in the wording of different audit reports.

A. THE SINGLE ENTITY

An Example

The audit report on a single company (which does not have subsidiaries) might currently read as follows:

> *To the Members of Any Company Limited*
> We have examined the accounts set out on pages x to y which have been prepared under the historical cost convention.
>
> In our opinion, the accounts give under the accounting convention described a true and fair view of the state of affairs of the Company at (date) and of the results and of the source and application of funds for the year ended on that date and comply with the Companies Acts 1948 and 1967.
>
> AN AUDITOR
> Place and date.

Addressee

The audit report is addressed to the "Members" of the company; the members are the shareholders of the company for the time being. The statutory requirement is that the audit report be addressed to them.[2] This is consistent with the statutory requirement that the directors submit the Accounts and the Directors' Report to shareholders.[3] Both the preparation of the accounts by the directors and the expression of an opinion on the accounts by the auditor relate to the discharge of obligations of accountability imposed on the directors and met in part by their duty to report to the shareholders. The auditor's judgment as to whether or not the accounts show a true and fair view of the resources and results of the enterprise has to be exercised from the point of view of "the members" (*ie* the shareholders) of the company.

The audit report, addressed to the shareholders of the reporting company should, therefore, confirm the validity of the directors' interpretation of the shareholders' perception of "a true and fair view". As has been discussed above, such an opinion includes consideration of the adequacy of the information and the lack of bias in its presentation, in the light of the use to be made of the information.

Within the apparently homogeneous (and distinguishable) interest group of shareholders there will be considerable differences in the personal objectives and interests of individuals. Each will have his personal perceptions, preferences and priorities which will be different from those of his fellows. If the perception of what constitutes a true and fair view is a matter of subjective judgment, then obviously the point of perception from which such judgment is exercised influences the conclusion as to whether or not a true and fair view has been disclosed. Accounts which give a true and fair view from the point of perception of shareholders as a group may well not give a true and fair view from the point of perception of lenders, nor from the points of perception of customers, suppliers, employees or other stakeholders. Accounts which give a true and fair view from the point of perception of shareholders as a group may not totally satisfy an individual shareholder's perception influenced by his own personal objectives.

Despite such conceptual difficulties, the audit opinion is regarded in practice as having significance and value to interest groups other than the collective group of shareholders to whom the audit report is addressed.

[2] Companies Act 1967, S. 14(1).
[3] Companies Act 1948, S. 158(1).

Although such other interests are not those explicitly addressed by the audit opinion, it nonetheless adds to the credibility, and thus to the utility, of the accounts for the non-shareholder users. Furthermore, information which is judged to be "true and fair" and thus, among other qualities, adequate and free from bias as judged from the point of view of shareholders is likely to represent useful and helpful (if insufficient) information for the purposes of lenders, employees, and others.

Scope of Opinion

The first paragraph of the opinion specifies the particular financial statements to which the audit opinion refers. The opinion embraces the statutorily required Profit and Loss Account, Balance Sheet and the Notes to both the Profit and Loss Account and to the Balance Sheet.[4] It also extends to the Statement of Source and Application of Funds which is not a statutory requirement but is called for by one of the Statements of Standard Accounting Practice[5] adopted by the accountancy profession.

These particular accounts and notes are the major vehicle of financial disclosure but are neither the only financial statements nor the only financial information contained in the company's Annual Report. The Directors' Report contains financial information, required either in compliance with statutory requirements,* or, for listed companies, with the requirements of the Stock Exchange. There is usually a section of statistical information, particularly summarised financial figures of the preceding five or more years. There will frequently be financial statements in a "Review of Operations" or in the Chairman's Statement or similar commentary. The audit opinion relates to and refers explicitly to the "formal" accounts, as defined in the previous paragraph, and not to the possibly extensive supplementary information elsewhere.

The auditor will do all he can to ensure that there should be no misunderstanding about the relevance or validity of his audit opinion which might arise from the context within which the audited accounts appear and particularly from the nature or content of unaudited financial statements

[4] Companies Act 1967, S. 14(1).

[5] SSAP No. 10.

*The statutory specification of items to be disclosed in the Directors' Report provides, with regard to certain matters, that, if the information is not provided by the directors, their omission must be made good by the auditor.[6] The very rare instances where the auditor thus provides specific information omitted from the Directors' Report do not necessarily imply a qualification to the audit opinion on the *accounts*.

[6] Companies Act 1967, Ss. 6, 7 & 8.

which appear in association with the audited accounts. The auditor will therefore satisfy himself that all other statements which are circulated within the same document or published at the same time as, and in association with, the audited accounts include figures which are identical to, or properly reconcilable with, those appearing in the audited accounts. He will ensure that any rearrangement, summarisation or analysis of audited figures does not distort the lack of bias which has been attained in the presentation of the audited "true and fair" accounts. He will reassure himself that any comment on the audited figures does not modify their significance, relevance or validity. The "other statements" which the auditor reviews for this purpose include the Directors' Report, Statistical Summaries, Review of Operations and Chairman's Statement.

The EEC 4th Directive requires the directors of a company to prepare and submit to shareholders an "Annual Report" which will, in some respects, go beyond the currently existing requirements of the UK statutorily-required Directors' Report: for example, information about likely future developments will be required.[7] The same Directive requires explicitly that the auditor satisfies himself that the annual report is consistent with the audited accounts.[8] The 4th Directive has not, at the time of writing, been incorporated into UK legislation, but when it is the consequent differences will be more of form than of substance. As explained above, the present UK practice is that auditors already consider and "approve" the contents of the Directors' Report as well as the figures appearing in other statements in the Company's Annual Report. Any legislative developments will tend to codify existing practice and eliminate any misunderstanding about the extent of the auditor's responsibility for the effect on users of statements appearing in the Directors' Report.

Measurement Method

In defining the accounts to which the audit opinion relates, reference is also made to the measurement system adopted. This is usually the historical cost convention (also called "historical cost basis of accounting"). This traditional financial convention uses a measurement system which is based on the historical cost of acquiring resources. The "capital" of the business entity is expressed in terms of the units of currency provided by the shareholders at the time they subscribed share capital and at the time of recognising retained profits. "Profit" is recognised as the excess of the monetary amount of resources attributable to shareholders at the end of the period

[7] EEC 4th Directive para 46.
[8] EEC 4th Directive para 51(1).

over the monetary amount attributable to shareholders at the start (adjusted as appropriate for payments to shareholders – *eg* dividends – and for receipts from them – *eg* new share subscriptions).

Recent experience of severe inflation has prompted renewed discussion of the adequacy or otherwise of the historical cost convention as a basis for financial statements. (Similar, inconclusive, discussion arose during the late 1940s and early 1950s). This has led to the issue in March 1980 of a Statement of Standard Accounting Practice calling for the preparation by most large "entities" (including companies) of financial statements on the basis of a current cost accounting ("CCA") system. (See SSAP No. 16 for details). Although the Standard, which is effective for accounting periods which *begin* on or after 1st January 1980, recognises that some companies may "wish to publish current cost accounts as their main or only accounts" (Part I – Explanatory Note para 28) it seems likely that, at least initially, CCA accounts will be regarded as *supplementary* to historical cost accounts (see, for example, paras 5 and 28 of Explanatory Note). For the time being there will be only a few exceptional companies which do not regard the historical cost accounts as the main accounts, and the historical cost convention will therefore be the usual measurement basis of a true and fair view.

In any event, in many individual cases a "pure" historical cost convention has already been modified by including in accounts some important items which are not measured on a basis of actual historical cost. Examples of such departures include some fixed assets (notably property stated at a valuation which is itself expressed in the monetary units of the time of valuation); items denominated in foreign currency (often expressed in the sterling equivalent of the foreign currency at the date of the balance sheet and not the sterling equivalent at the date of the foreign currency transaction); and some investments in the shares of other companies (notably associated companies but also some portfolio investments).

Despite doubts about the validity of a measurement system based on historical cost it is important to recognise certain positive attributes. It may well partly provide a useful measure of the effectiveness of the exercise of "stewardship". Because the measurement system is directly related to actual cash values of real transactions, the implied concept of capital allows shareholders to assure themselves that the *cash* value of their interest in the resources of the business is being preserved. Creditors, whether for goods, services, or finance, whose claims are almost universally expressed in contemporaneously current monetary units (unadjusted for the impact of inflation) can discern the extent of security for discharge of sums due to them. The characteristics of the convention mean that transactions-based measurements are objectively verifiable. (Judgment, of course, follows measurement through the accounting process in the application of such concepts as "matching" and "prudence", referred to in Section 1). The historical cost convention is likely to have relevance if only for limited specific purposes. Authority for the current continuing use of the convention can be found in statements by the professional accountancy societies. In early 1976, in the midst of lively debate about accounting bases, these societies issued a guidance statement[9] emphasising the impossibility, for the time being at least, of identifying any single, uniquely appropriate, accounting basis. The Statement also emphasised the importance of specifying explicitly the measurement convention adopted. Hence the specific reference in the example referred to.*

Experiments with alternative bases of financial measurement can be expected to continue. Since the mid-1970s attention has focussed on systems of "Current Cost Accounting" (CCA). This basis of financial measurement attributes to the resources of the business accounting values which represent the "value to the business" of the items concerned. This will usually be equivalent to the cost of replacing the item. The "capital" of the business is represented by the current cost of the resources provided. In general terms, CCA profits charge against current sales revenues not the historical costs of acquiring resources consumed in generating that revenue, but the current cost (usually measured by the replacement cost). A relatively small number of companies, but some of the largest, have already reported supplementary CCA results and it is likely that both the extent of CCA information provided and the number of companies providing it will increase under the stimulus of the recent Statement of Standard Accounting Practice.[10]

In a number of cases to date the (supplementary) CCA accounts have also been reported on by the auditor, usually either by extension of the "basic" audit opinion relating to the historical cost accounts or by a separate report related specifically to the CCA statements. The appropriate terms of audit report on CCA accounts (if any) are still under discussion but, obviously, any CCA-related audit report should make clear the extent of validation, if

[9] CCAB Guidance Statement "Inflation Accounting – the interim period". (Hyde Guidelines).

* The explicit reference to the accounting convention is not to be seen as a "qualification" to the audit opinion. Since it is for the directors to specify the convention on which the accounts are based, the Statement of Accounting Policies (called for by Statement of Standard Accounting Practice – SSAP 2) often begins by stating the accounting convention. A reference in the audit opinion in such cases to the Accounting Policies thus covers reference to the accounting convention.

[10] SSAP 16.

any, being provided by the auditor. The absence of an explicit audit report on CCA accounts does not imply an adverse opinion. On the contrary, an "unaudited" CCA statement is one further example of an additional financial statement which is not embraced by the explicit terms of the audit report and thus it falls within the auditor's review for credibility and for consistency with the audited accounts (as explained above). In the absence of any explicit adverse report, therefore, the user of financial statements can assume that the CCA accounts have been prepared in an appropriate manner and restate the historical cost-based information in terms appropriate to the representation of financial results and resources on the basis of the CCA convention.

When, as is to be expected under SSAP 16, a relatively large number of companies are preparing and publishing both historical cost and CCA financial statements, how is the auditor to report? Some argue that at the present evolutionary stage of CCA reporting it is inappropriate to offer a "true and fair" opinion on CCA accounts; others suggest that the "true and fair" opinion on the historical cost accounts can be simply extended to embrace the related CCA accounts. One point at least is clear: if a company within the scope of SSAP 16 fails to prepare and publish the required CCA accounts, the auditor will draw attention in his opinion to the company's failure to comply with those requirements. Such failure to provide CCA information, however, will not of itself affect the validity of the true and fair view presented by the historical cost accounts which may well be validated by an unqualified audit opinion.

It is possible that the CCA financial statements will be the only ones published, or will be the main financial statements, with (and possibly in isolated instances even without) a statement reconciling key CCA figures to the historical cost accounts. It is generally accepted that CCA financial statements are capable of giving a true and fair view according to that specific accounting convention. Certainly the Board of any company in the UK which published only CCA financial statements – and there have been a very small number of instances – must believe that they can thereby discharge their legal obligations (to prepare accounts giving a true and fair view). Recent statements of the accountancy profession lend credence to this proposition, and those auditors who have to date given unqualified audit opinions on the limited number of instances to date of CCA accounts without historical cost figures have clearly satisfied themselves on the point. Some commentators go as far as to suggest that in current inflationary conditions historical cost financial statements cannot give a true and fair view and they challenge the legality of such accounts. However, historical cost accounts – alone or supplemented by CCA figures – are still and will, for some time, continue to be the usual form, and auditors, on the whole, do not express opinions other than that such accounts do show a true and fair view.

Sometimes the scope paragraph will refer to the company's stated accounting policies (see the footnote to page 24). The auditor will certainly consider carefully the detailed accounting policies adopted by the company, even if they are not explicitly referred to in his report. He will ensure that they are properly detailed and disclosed by the directors in the context of the accounts or in the notes embraced by his opinion.[12] An unqualified audit opinion will imply the auditor's concurrence with the accounting policies selected and applied by the directors, but not a qualitative judgment about whether they are the "best". (See pages 13 and 14).

The Opinion

The existence of his opinion in written, public form imposes on the auditor onerous professional, legal, and social responsibilities. The audit report exemplified above contains, as its second paragraph, what is commonly referred to as the opinion paragraph. This expresses the professional opinion of the auditor. To be eligible for appointment the auditor has to be a member of one of the four professional accountancy societies in the UK specified in company law.[13] Membership of a professional society involves lengthy study, training and experience. (There are transitional arrangements to protect the rights of long-established "unqualified" auditors and also special arrangements for recognising overseas qualifications). Each accountancy society imposes professional obligations on its members and thus on the individual auditor, who is exposed to the hazard of professional disciplinary proceedings as well as to the process of law.

The audit report expresses an audit opinion on two significant matters. Firstly, it confirms the auditor's opinion that the accounts do give a true and fair view (of the state of affairs, of the profit and of the source and application of funds of the company). Secondly, it confirms that statutory requirements have been complied with; these are the specific disclosure requirements set out in the Companies Acts 1948 and 1967. Of course, the over-riding statutory requirement is that the profit and loss account and balance sheet should show a true and fair view of the results and state of affairs of the company; explicit reference in the audit opinion to the attainment of this objective emphasises its predominance. The way in which these two elements of the audit opinion are expressed distinguishes the primary requirement

[12] SSAP No 2.
[13] Companies Act 1976, S. 13(1).

that accounts show a true and fair view from the subordinate requirement that they comply with specific detailed disclosure provisions. (The relationship of detailed statutory disclosure requirements to the overall true and fair view was explored in Section I).

From the point of view of audit, the statutory disclosure requirements impose an absolute duty on the company. The audit opinion on this aspect therefore relates only to whether compliance has been achieved or not and is not a qualitative opinion about the nature of the disclosed item; nor is the audit opinion with regard to compliance with disclosure requirements concerned with materiality. There should be relatively little difficulty in arriving at a conclusion with regard to this element of the audit opinion because whether there is or is not a transaction or item which falls within the defined disclosure requirements will usually be a matter of fact. Quantification of such transactions or items will usually be relatively straightforward. (Difficulties of quantification will, of course, arise from time to time – for example, the evaluation of individual components of the "package" of Directors' emoluments – and in extreme cases, when "proper accounting records" have not been maintained, it is unlikely that any opinion can be offered about individual disclosure of specific items).

That part of the audit opinion which relates to the true and fair view is both fundamental and more difficult. The opinion as to the existence of a true and fair view is the heart of the audit report and implies other conclusions which will be referred to separately in Section 4. The brief discussion earlier (Section 2) of the true and fair view is essential to an understanding of the significance of the audit opinion in this regard.

The processes of financial measurement and of financial disclosure depend upon the exercise of judgment; the process of audit examination similarly depends upon the exercise of different, independent, judgment. It must be emphasised, therefore, that the audit opinion confirms the existence of *a* true and fair view and not *the* true and fair view. It should also be clear from the discussion up to this point that the auditor's assessment of the validity of the financial statements has to be made from the perception of shareholders, they being but one group among many now identified as interested in receiving and using the information contained in audited accounts. The audit opinion relates to financial statements and is therefore obviously constrained by the limitations to the processes of accounting measurement and reporting. Because of these limitations and those of the processes of auditing, audited accounts are not "correct" in any sense implying some concept of unique validity or of universal relevance.

The audit opinion refers explicitly to the state of affairs of the company at the balance sheet date. The balance sheet can be thought of as being in the nature of a snapshot – it portrays at a particular point of time the disposition of the resources of the business and of claims on those resources. In the dynamic environment of business activity, the disposition of resources, and of claims, is constantly changing. The balance sheet should portray the position as at the date on which it is prepared; it is not representative of the state of affairs *throughout* the period since the previous balance sheet. The financial position represented by the balance sheet reflects subsequent knowledge to the extent to which that is relevant in defining financial measurement and disclosure. The balance sheet is not a statement of value; the over-riding accountancy concept of prudence recognises claims on resources more readily than the existence of resources; the historical cost convention uses the completed rather than the hypothetical transaction as the basis of financial measurement.

The unqualified audit opinion validates and confirms the discharge by the directors (and on their behalf, by management) of record-keeping and financial reporting obligations. The unqualified opinion is a strong indication of management's desire to meet its obligations to shareholders. Audit consideration of the effectiveness of accounting and control systems and of evidence of compliance with specified procedures will add to audit assurance of the completeness (are all the transactions recorded?) and accuracy (are transactions recorded correctly?) of recording individual transactions. The audit opinion, however, relates explicitly and exclusively to specified accounts.

Authentication

The illustrative example above (p. 19) demonstrates that the audit report is always signed as evidence and authentication of the opinion expressed. Signatures will usually be printed on copies but there will always exist one copy (or a small number of copies) of the audit report and the accounts to which it relates with actual manuscript signatures.[14] The common practice of audit appointments being made in the name of a firm means that the audit report is usually signed in the firm's name. The auditor's signature in such cases will be the firm's name subscribed by an individual partner acting on behalf of himself and all his partners in the firm; all partners share responsibility for the opinion expressed in the firm's name under which they practise together. The auditor may, of course, be appointed individually, in

[14] The copy lodged with the Registrar of Companies requires manuscript signatures – Companies Act 1976, S. 1(7).

which case the audit opinion will be signed by the individual practitioner. If that individual practitioner is also a partner in an audit firm, it is unlikely that his fellow partners will escape responsibility by association for the opinion which he expresses in his own name.

The place of signing the audit report is also recorded. This is usually the town in which the particular audit firm is based, or, in the case of a firm with many offices, the town which is the base of the partner or partners to whom has been allocated prime responsibility for discharging the firm's audit obligations for the particular company. This will usually be the location of the audit firm's office most conveniently situated to the company's head office.

Date

The audit report is dated when the audit report is actually signed. This will obviously be between the date to which the financial statements have been prepared, and the date of the company's General meeting to which the audited accounts will be submitted. Therefore the sequence of events, after the financial statements have been completed by the company's management and after detailed audit work has been completed, should be:–

approval of the accounts by the Board;

signature of the accounts by two directors, on behalf of all directors, which formally witnesses Board approval;

completion of the audit report by signature.

It is becoming increasingly common practice for the auditor (or a partner representing his firm) to attend the Board meeting at which the accounts are formally approved and for him to be present when the two directors sign the accounts. The "accounts" approved by the Board will include the final version of the Directors' Report and other statements for which directors are individually and collectively responsible. When this procedure is followed, therefore, the auditor is also able to assure himself finally about the context in which the audited accounts will be submitted to and read by the users. The auditor then signs the audit report on the manually signed copy or copies. Whatever the detailed arrangements adopted, the auditor should not authenticate his opinion by signature until the Board has approved the accounts and these have been signed by two directors. The directors are responsible for the accounts; the auditor is responsible for his opinion on the accounts.

As already noted, the balance sheet is drawn up to show the state of affairs of the company at a specific date. This date is inevitably prior to that on which the audit report is signed. It is therefore essential to carry out a review of major events and transactions which have occurred between the balance sheet date and the date on which the audit report is signed to confirm that there have been no significant transactions or events which invalidate any of the bases on which the audited accounts were prepared.

Frequently this audit review of post-balance sheet events serves to confirm the validity of the accounts, but other cases do sometimes arise. (Although some aspects of such cases will now be considered in some detail it should not be thought that this is a subject of frequent audit difficulty). One example might be the intervention of insolvency, which means that the going concern basis of accounts (see page 16), which seemed valid at the balance sheet date, is no longer appropriate. Post-balance sheet date events may prompt some re-assessment of the previously made quantification of resources, or of claims on resources, as they existed at the balance sheet date. A distinction is drawn between events which are "adjustable" – that is, those which prompt re-assessment and re-statement of the financial figures – and "non-adjustable" – that is, those for which disclosure of the event is appropriate without necessarily requiring re-measurement or re-statement of items in the accounts.* Similar considerations, of course, also arise for the profit and loss account.

The validity of the accounts is obviously a function of the date at which they are prepared, because that date defines the information available as a basis for the exercise of the judgment needed in their preparation. The date on which the financial statements are approved by the directors is the date on which they are formally approved by the Board. Financial statements cannot be approved "as at" some earlier, notional, date. Similarly, the audit opinion is time-critical in that the date at which it is expressed determines the nature and extent of the evidence available as a basis for the opinion. The date of the audit report determines the date of expression of opinion. The date of the opinion should be the actual date of signature – the audit report should not be pre-dated nor post-dated. Events which have occurred prior to the date of signing fall within the range of possible knowledge or evidence

*Discussion of post-balance sheet date events and the distinction between adjustable and non-adjustable items will be found in the appropriate Statement of Standard Accounting Practice, (at the time of writing, ED 22, which will become SSAP No. 17).

available to the auditor in formulating his opinion. Unless there were prior indications or expectation, events which occur after the date of signing will not normally be available as evidence in formulating the audit opinion.

In addition to the time "gap" between the balance sheet date and the date of signing the audit report, another important "gap" is the interval between signing the audit report and the date of the company's Annual General Meeting at which the audited accounts are formally submitted to shareholders. This period can be thought of as consisting of two stages:–

(i) between the date of signing the audit report and the date of circulating the accounts to shareholders with notice of the meeting; and

(ii) between the date of circulating the accounts and the meeting itself.

It is clearly the responsibility of the directors to ensure that they lay before shareholders accounts which represent a true and fair view of the results and resources of the company for a period and at a time in the past. The directors have to ensure that the accounts do reflect all information relevant to the financial measurement of items in the accounts. It is, therefore, the directors' duty to disclose to shareholders either prior to, or in extreme cases at, the General Meeting all relevant facts and events which may have emerged subsequent to the signing of the audit report and which influence either the accounts themselves or the shareholders' perception of them. In an extreme case the directors would "withdraw" the initial audited accounts and decline to submit them in their original form to the shareholders. An adjourned Annual General Meeting would in due course receive the amended accounts, audited of course.

As already noted, the date of the audit opinion determines the extent of the auditor's possible knowledge. It thus influences a subsequent view of the degree of diligence with which audit responsibilities have been discharged. The auditor probably cannot "withdraw" an audit report, although there have been instances where auditors have purported to do so. The position is by no means clear; for example, some commentators seek to distinguish circumstances where auditors may have been negligent in their search for or interpretation of evidence from those in which their diligence has been frustrated by suppression or falsification of evidence. What follows represents a personal viewpoint. If he subsequently acquires evidence or information which indicates that the signed audit opinion has become invalid, his reporting obligations can only be discharged by the auditor informing the directors of the additional evidence and of the respect in which it now appears to him that the accounts fail to show a true and fair view. The directors, in turn, have a duty to convey this information to the shareholders. (In certain circumstances the auditor may wish to supplement information from the directors with his own statement of the position). If the directors were to decline to convey the subsequently discovered information to the shareholders, then the auditor would have an opportunity to do so at the Annual General Meeting. He receives notice of General Meetings and has the right to be present and the right to be heard on the accounts.[15] In the unusual circumstances in which it might be appropriate, the auditor must make clear that the opinion which he held at the date on which he signed his audit report is no longer valid.

B. THE PARENT COMPANY*

An Example

The audit report on the consolidated accounts of a parent company and its subsidiaries typically reads as follows:–

> *To the Members of Any Parent Company Limited*
> We have examined the accounts set out on pages x to y which have been prepared under the historical cost convention modified to include the revaluation of certain properties.
>
> In our opinion the accounts give, under the accounting convention stated above and *so far as concerns the members of the Company*,+ a true and fair view of the state of affairs of the Company and of the Group at (date) and of the profit and source and application of funds

[15] Companies Act 1967, S. 14(7).

*United Kingdom parlance uses "parent company" and "holding company" as virtually synonymous. The wording of the relevant statutory enactments refers to a "holding company".[16] Sometimes the phrase "parent company" implies the idea of "ultimate holding company" – that is, the pinnacle of a corporate structure in which the "holding company" has subsidiaries which are themselves holding companies of sub-subsidiaries. In certain limited circumstances such subsidiary holding companies are not required to prepare and submit group accounts. Therefore the phrase "parent company" has been used throughout the discussion which follows to mean the reporting entity. (It should be noted that UK usage of the phrase "holding company" is different from USA usage).

[16] Companies Act 1948, S. 154.

+See page 33

of the Group for the 52 weeks ended on that date and comply with the Companies Acts 1948 and 1967.

AN AUDITOR

Place and Date

The significant difference in wording as compared with the single entity s in italics for emphasis:

"*So far as concerns the members of the Company*".+

Characteristics of Group Accounts

This phrase occurs in an audit report on group accounts which consolidate the accounts of the parent company with those of its subsidiaries. Consolidated accounts are not a simple aggregation of the accounts of the parent company and its subsidiaries, but incorporate certain consolidation adjustments. The group of companies – parent and subsidiaries together – is effectively regarded as an extension of the parent company. The group accounts, therefore, represent the consolidated results and resources of the economic entity comprised by the group as a whole as if that group were in reality also a single legal entity. Consolidated accounts are prepared from the point of view of the shareholders in the parent company. The auditor of the parent company of a group reports to the shareholders of the parent company on the consolidated accounts of the group as a whole. These obviously incorporate the accounts of the parent company itself as a separate entity. (But it should be noted that only the Balance Sheet of the parent company appears along with the Consolidated Balance Sheet of the group, the parent company Profit and Loss Account is usually "incorporated" within the single Consolidated Profit and Loss Account of the group).

A group of companies within which the share capital of the subsidiaries is not owned or controlled entirely by the parent will have minority interests, representing "outside" interests or participations in individual subsidiary companies. The figure which appears in the consolidated group accounts for "Minority Interests", however, does not necessarily represent the claims of such minorities on the total resources of the group. Minorities have no direct interest in the group as a whole because, by definition, their interest is not expressed through membership of the parent company; their interests are expressed in and through the particular subsidiary company in which they participate directly as shareholders. Minority interests of the group must look to the accounts of the particular subsidiary in which they participate to

+Some auditors regard the additional phrase identified above as being inferred by the relevant legislation and therefore omit it from their audit report.

disclose a true and fair view of its individual results and resources, and assess thereby the extent of their claims on the results and resources of the subsidiary – not of the group. The auditor of the subsidiary, of course, reports his opinion on its accounts to its shareholders, who obviously include the group and the minority interests.

Other Auditors

Groups are frequently organised in such a way that different auditors are responsible for the audits of individual constituent companies. The auditor of the parent company need not necessarily audit the accounts of all the subsidiaries. (There are extreme cases where the parent company auditor does not audit directly any of the subsidiaries). However, the auditor of the parent company always has total responsibility for reporting on the consolidated group accounts. He cannot evade or modify that responsibility because he does not audit directly all constituent member companies of the group, nor can he seek to share that responsibility with the auditors of any individual subsidiaries.

It is, however, regarded as important that the shareholders of the parent company should be informed of the extent to which subsidiaries have their accounts audited other than by the auditors of the parent company. The professional accountancy societies have accordingly recommended that the directors of the parent company identify those group companies which are not audited by the parent company auditor.[17] This recommendation is not always followed. Some audit reports on group accounts refer explicitly to the fact that "the accounts of certain subsidiaries have been audited by other auditors", or incorporate wording to the same effect. This wording is sometimes used to reinforce the information provided by the parent company directors about group audit arrangements, and sometimes to rectify their failure to provide such information. The absence from the audit report of such a phrase does not necessarily imply "consolidated audit" (that is all companies in the group audited by the same auditor) by the parent company auditor. Some auditors argue that, if the directors of the parent company decline to disclose information about the audit of group companies, it is not for the auditors to inform the parent company shareholders; it is suggested that such reference by auditors may confuse and be misunderstood as being an audit qualification. In any event it is clear that a phrase about "other auditors" in the audit opinion on group accounts is neither a qualification nor a restriction of scope of either examination or opinion.

[17] See, for example, The Institute of Chartered Accountants of Scotland Statement on Auditing No 4 "Group Accounts – Reliance on Other Auditors" para 23.

The auditor of the parent company has to ensure that the accounts of subsidiaries have been compiled on bases which are consistent with the accounting policies adopted by the parent company. As noted earlier, consolidated group accounts are more than an aggregation of the figures appearing in the audited accounts of constituent companies and consolidate the individual companies' accounts together with such other information and adjustments as are required to ensure that the consolidated accounts provide a true and fair view of the results and resources of the group as a whole. (Examples of consolidating adjustments are those arising on changes in the composition of the group and the elimination of unrealised profits in stocks of group origin). Subsidiaries therefore must provide figures which can be consolidated in such a way that the group accounts do show a true and fair view of the results and resources of the total group (parent company and subsidiaries taken together). The auditor of the parent company also has to satisfy himself that the audit evidence – tests and techniques – used by other auditors in arriving at their opinions on the accounts of individual subsidiaries do support the opinion expressed by the parent company auditor on the consolidated group accounts.

The auditor of the parent company will not necessarily have investigated the accounts of a subsidiary directly, unless, obviously, he also audits that subsidiary. Therefore, in considering the validity of the information provided by the subsidiary for the purposes of consolidation the parent company auditor must decide to what extent he can rely on the opinion of the subsidiary auditor or, conversely, to what extent he requires to examine directly the subsidiary's accounts. This decision will be influenced, at least in part, by the impression gained by the parent company auditor of the effectiveness of control over financial reporting within the group itself and of the efficiency and effectiveness of the audit work on which the subsidiary auditor based his opinion. As a matter of professional practice the parent company auditor will normally seek explanations and information from the various auditors of subsidiary companies. Such information commonly extends to a review by the parent company auditor of the files and working papers of the subsidiary company auditor. Recent legislation[18] specifies that an auditor of a subsidiary company has a duty to give to the auditor of the parent company such information and explanation as may reasonably be required for the purpose of the audit of the group accounts.

Subsidiaries in overseas locations present particular problems. Controls within the group itself may be less stringent or less effective than those on "domestic" subsidiaries. The overseas subsidiary's local auditor may not share

[18] Companies Act 1976, S. 18(1a).

the same perceptions of audit objectives and processes as the UK-based parent company auditor. The overseas auditor may very well belong to a local accountancy society and thus not be subject to the same professional and legal jurisdiction as the parent company auditor. Recognising those difficulties, UK company law[19] places on the directors of the parent company itself the responsibility for ensuring that the parent company auditor obtains all the information needed about an overseas subsidiary's accounts and audit.

C. THE AUDITING STANDARD

The Consultative Committee of Accountancy Bodies ("C.C.A.B.") comprises the six major accountancy societies in the UK and its Auditing Practices Committee ("A.P.C.") consists of representatives of the four CCAB accountancy societies whose members are recognised as qualified to act as auditors (see Section 5, page 47). In 1978, APC published an initial series of Discussion Drafts of Auditing Standards and Guidelines which led ultimately to the simultaneous publication in April 1980 by the four individual professional societies concerned of the first Auditing Standards and Guidelines. The Explanatory Foreword makes clear (para 11) that "members of the (relevant) accountancy bodies who assume responsibility as auditors are expected to observe Auditing Standards" on pain of appropriate disciplinary procedures. One of the first Auditing Standards dealt with the Audit Report. The text is reproduced in Appendix I and some brief comments follow.

The Standard Audit Report

The Auditing Standard dealing with the Audit Report proposes (para 11) the following wording as illustrative of an Audit Report which would comply with the Standard:

> *Auditors' report to the members of any company limited*
> We have audited the financial statements on pages x to y *in accordance with approved Auditing Standards.*
>
> In our opinion the financial statements, which have been prepared under the historical cost convention as modified by the revaluation of land and buildings, give a true and fair view of the state of the company's affairs at (date) and of its profit and source and application of

[19] Companies Act 1976, S. 18(1b).

funds for the year then ended and comply with the Companies Acts 1948 and 1967.

AN AUDITOR

Place

Date

The significantly different words are again in italics.

The Draft Auditing Standard

The introduction to this Section made clear that the choice of wording of the audit report is, of course, ultimately dependent on the decision of the auditor. Publication of Auditing Standards does not alter that individual professional responsibility.

The text of the Auditing Standard for the Audit Report is short. The sections most directly relevant to the present discussion are paragraphs 2 and 3 which are quoted in full:

"2. The audit report should identify those to whom it is addressed and the financial statements to which it relates.

3. The auditor should refer expressly in his report to the following:

(a) whether the financial statements have been audited in accordance with approved Auditing Standards;

(b) whether in the auditor's opinion the financial statements give a true and fair view of the state of affairs, profit or loss and, where applicable, source and application of funds; and

(c) any matters prescribed by relevant legislation or other requirements."

With the one significant exception of the matter of sub-paragraph 3(a) all these points are already dealt with explicitly in the current wording of audit reports (see p. 19). The phrases identified above deal with the new material introduced in the illustrative Audit Report to cover sub-paragraph 3(a) of the Auditing Standard.

As noted in Sections A and B above, the usual form of audit report issued hitherto does not refer explicitly to "approved Auditing Standards". Of course, none of these formerly existed in the sense in which the phrase is now used to mean a document codifying conduct and procedures. There have certainly always been "auditing standards" (with a small 's'). These uncodified auditing standards are those which are perceived by the individual auditor as appropriate to the completion of his audit task.

The effect of progressive codification of Auditing Standards should not therefore be misunderstood; they do not modify the auditor's personal professional responsibility to maintain audit standards (small 's'). Indeed, the Explanatory Foreword (para 4) emphasises the point thus:–

> "In the observance of Auditing Standards, therefore, the auditor must exercise his judgement in determining both the auditing procedures necessary in the circumstances to afford a reasonable basis for his opinion and the wording of his report".

The chairman of APC introducing the "new Auditing Standards" in a letter published in the APC quarterly bulletin True and Fair (No 15, Spring 1980) provided the following personal gloss:

> "Auditing Standards and Guidelines are, of course, only the codification of existing best practice. That is not to suggest that Auditing Standards and Guidelines can ever replace the judgement of the individual member [auditor] ".

The omission up to the present of any explicit reference in the audit report to "Auditing Standards" should not therefore be misunderstood. The audit opinion as expressed at present implies the existence of individually perceived auditing standards. Without such personally defined auditing standards there would be no basis for the subjective professional judgement which is contained in the audit opinion.

Each individual auditor's perception of appropriate standards is influenced by his knowledge of developments within three communities – (i) society at large, (ii) the professional accountancy society and (iii) individual audit firms (his own and others). Reports of legal decisions in Court cases provide indications of social perceptions of developing auditing standards. So too do the published Reports of Department of Trade Inspectors as well as comment in the general and professional press. Professional statements, guidance notes, disciplinary procedures and articles in the professional press provide indications of changing perceptions within the accountancy profession of what constitute appropriate auditing standards. Auditing Standards and Guidelines now contribute to professionally-originated information. Personal and professional contacts are a source of information about how individual audit firms and auditors are developing their perceptions of auditing standards.

An original (1978) draft version of the Auditing Standards proposed the inclusion in the audit report of an express statement confirming that the auditor had carried out "such procedures as he considered necessary". Some argued that explicit inclusion of this phrase helped to emphasise the subjective nature of the determination of the work to be done as a basis for the audit opinion; others that its use was unnecessary. The present terms of the audit opinion, they argued, already imply that the audit examination complies with the procedures which the auditor considers necessary as a basis for his opinion. What these procedures typically include will be referred to later in Section 7. There now follows reference to some other implications of the audit report – what it means without expressly saying so.

4 *What Else the Audit Report Means*

The foregoing discussion of the explicit terms of the unqualified audit report has already indicated clearly that it has important implied terms. These can be considered under two broad headings:

(a) those which arise from the statutorily-defined obligations of the auditor; and

(b) those which arise from the practical organisation and completion of audit work.

Statutory Implications

In addition to an explicit affirmative report on certain matters, UK statute law requires the auditor to report on other matters by exception.[1] That means that explicit reference in the audit report is needed only if a presumed state of affairs does not exist. Three specific "statutory presumptions" which the unqualified audit opinion tacitly confirms are:

(i) that proper accounting records ("books of account") have been kept by the company;

(ii) that the balance sheet and the profit and loss account are in agreement with the books of account;

(iii) that the auditor obtained all the information and explanations which, to the best of his knowledge and belief, were necessary for the purposes of his audit.

[1] Companies Act 1967, S. 14.

.The auditor, therefore, has a statutorily imposed duty to come to a conclusion on these points and to carry out such examination and obtain such evidence as he needs to allow him to form an opinion on them.

Obviously, an auditor could not form any opinion at all if he were forced to conclude that he had not received all the information and explanations he thought he required. Similarly, if an auditor were to conclude that proper accounting records had not been kept, he would be precluded from expressing an unqualified opinion on the accounts derived from these accounting records. Proper accounting records are defined as those which will permit a true and fair view to be derived from them.[2] It is, therefore, obvious that if the accounts are to show a true and fair view such records will have been maintained.

The statutory definition of proper accounting records implies that they are properly maintained. It also implies that appropriate controls exist and are operated to ensure that the realities of business transactions are reflected in the financial records. The unqualified audit opinion, therefore, implies a favourable conclusion about the existence and operation of accounting and managerial controls.

Practical Implications

As explained later, in Section 6, the auditor's work in establishing the existence of systems of control, and in evaluating their effectiveness in design and implementation, is a fundamental part of the audit evidence on which his opinion is based.

Other implications of the unqualified audit report derive from the nature of the audit process and from audit practice. These can be considered as:

compliance of accounts with Accounting Standards, and with the Stock Exchange Listing Agreement

compliance of accounts with certain detailed legal restrictions

consistency of audit work with auditing standards and "guidelines" (note the small letters!)

[2] Companies Act 1976, S. 12.

observation of Auditing Standards and consideration of Auditing Guidelines

the expectation of absence of significant undetected errors.

Accounting Standards are promulgated by the major UK professional accountancy societies, including those whose members are qualified to act as auditors. The accountancy societies require all their members (including, obviously, those members who act as auditors) to ensure that accounts are prepared in compliance with Statements of Standard Accounting Practice ("SSAPs") because it is expected that compliance with SSAPs will usually be consistent with attaining the objective of giving a true and fair view. SSAPs are therefore seen as being more prescriptive than "guidelines" or "norms", and those issued to date specify various matters relating to financial measurement, accounting treatment and financial disclosure. They usually identify one or a very restricted number of procedures as the "Standard" method. In the absence of any specific reference in the audit report, there is an implication that the accounts have been drawn up in conformity with the appropriate SSAPs.* (See also paragraph 6 of the Audit Report Auditing Standard, reproduced in Appendix I.)

A company listed on the UK Stock Exchange has to comply with the disclosure requirements of the Listing Agreement, which in some detailed respects go beyond statutory requirements. There is no formal obligation on the auditor to report in this regard and there is no *locus* for him so to report even if his opinion were that the directors had not discharged their obligations in this regard. The directors have direct responsibility to the Stock Exchange in consequence of their acceptance of the obligations of the Listing Agreement, but the auditor is not a party to that agreement. However, he will, as a professional person, assist the directors to ensure that they have discharged their responsibilities. In practice, therefore, it can be assumed that the auditor has considered the Stock Exchange disclosure requirements,

*There may be, probably unusual, circumstances where the auditor agrees with the directors that the attainment of the true and fair view demands departure from an SSAP; if so, there will be a clear indication in the accounts of that fact and of the consequences of departure. The audit opinion will include at present a specific statement of the auditor's concurrence with the departure. There is, currently, discussion about the significance or relevance of explicit concurrence by the auditor in such non-compliance. It is suggested that the audit opinion confirming the existence of a true and fair view in circumstances where the accounts make clear the fact and significance of departure from any SSAP implies concurrence in the departure by the auditor. If he did not concur, he would be unable to express an unqualified opinion.

where these are relevant, and has satisfied himself that they have been met by the company.

If the accounts are to show a true and fair view they will have to make clear the potential financial consequences of exceeding the formal powers of the company. The auditor will therefore have to consider whether any transactions may have been undertaken beyond the constraints imposed by the company's Memorandum and Articles of Association. Breaches of the terms of the Memorandum are likely to be substantially legalistic, to occur only rarely and to be confined to the objects clause. There may be little, if any, financial consequence, but such a breach may provide significant indication of lack of control, or of discipline, in the arrangements for conducting the affairs of the company. An auditor would therefore have to consider whether such a breach required action beyond bringing it to the attention of the directors for them to consider how the matter should be resolved. Similarly with a breach of the terms of the Articles of Association, it may be sufficient to ensure that the directors are aware of the breach and that they remedy its consequences. However, breach of the Articles may involve financial consequences which should be disclosed in the accounts, and since the Articles regulate the conduct of directors (as opposed to the company as a corporate entity), a breach of their provisions may be a more serious indication of inadequate control and discipline in the management of corporate affairs with consequent implications for the nature and extent of evidence which the auditor seeks. In an extreme case, where the auditor felt that the outcome was significant either in terms of financial consequence or in its implications for the good governance of the company, he would probably ensure that appropriate disclosure was made.

Any financial statements showing a true and fair view should disclose the existence and amount of significant actual, potential, and contingent liabilities which are relevant to the true and fair view. Obviously, accounts which show a true and fair view will disclose the existence of significant liabilities, including those which derive from legal consequences – civil or criminal. If no such liabilities are disclosed, the implication is that none exists – the company's resources are not in hazard from breaches of the law. If they exist and are not disclosed, the accounts do not show a true and fair view. Where certain company transactions may have penal consequences, it will be necessary to consider the appropriate financial measurement and disclosure of the potentially adverse consequences. Breach of statutory restrictions will also be disclosed even if non-disclosure is not fundamental to a true and fair view. The audit opinion that the accounts show a true and fair view, therefore, implies that the auditor has considered the question of such liabilities.*

In their statements the professional bodies distinguish between "Standards" and the "Guidelines" which support or amplify them. APC Standards would "apply whenever an audit is carried out" and prescribe basic principles and practices. Earlier discussion in Section 3 C, distinguished the current conventional wording of the audit report from that now illustrated in the Auditing Standards and the difference between "Auditing Standards" (capitals) and "auditing standards" (small letters). It has already been explained that the unqualified audit report implies that the auditor's examination has met the standards of skill and care which would currently be generally expected of an audit practitioner.

Auditing Guidelines give "guidance on procedures by which the Auditing Standards may be applied . . ."; they "do not prescribe basic principles and practices". An Auditing Guideline effectively raises a presumption that in normal circumstances the auditor will have had regard to it in completing his audit examination. The auditor will not necessarily always follow the Guideline, but he will have to satisfy himself that in the particular circumstances of the audit assignment there were better audit tests or more appropriate audit work which meant he should follow procedures other than those indicated in the Guideline. "Auditing Guidelines" for the conduct of audit work already exist in Guidance Statements published by the individual professional accountancy bodies. These "guidelines" and other professional statements are seen as providing assistance to the auditor by providing him with an outline of a normal approach for dealing with particular audit situations.

If a problem with regard to the audit opinion were subsequently to emerge, the ultimate test of the validity and appropriateness of audit work actually carried out would always be judicial process before the Courts.

*This paragraph touches on difficult and unresolved issues, some of which are referred to superficially later, in Section 9. Some commentators believe that the auditor cannot be expected to act almost as guarantor of good behaviour by the company and its directors for either one or both of two reasons. They argue that it is impracticable to expect the auditor to know enough about all the potential failures and/or that it is unrealistic to impose on the auditor the responsibilities of acting as "policeman" and that to do so would change fundamentally the auditor/company roles. (See, for example, The Institute of Chartered Accountants of Scotland Statement of Professional Conduct "Unlawful Acts or Defaults by Clients of Members"). Others assert that the modern auditor acts as the custodian of the corporate conscience and that a significant social role of the auditor is to help the management (principally the directors) of the company to display their discharge of the responsibilities of "good citizenship".

The Explanatory Note to the Auditing Standards and Guidelines makes clear (para 7) that in "considering the adequacy of the work of an auditor [a court of law may] take into account any pronouncements or publications which it thinks may be indicative of good practice. Auditing Standards and Guidelines are likely to be so regarded." Additionally, or alternatively, the auditor will face the hazards of the investigation and disciplinary procedures of the accountancy profession through his membership of a particular Institute or Association.

Subject to inevitable limits of materiality and of confidence (which were discussed also in Section 3), audited accounts should not include undetected errors. There is and can be no *certainty* that this is so. The audit task has to be completed within practical constraints of time and of cost. It is not feasible to examine every transaction or document; certainty is unattainable. There are no universally understood or accepted criteria by which to quantify limits of materiality or of degrees of confidence. However, by and large and within limits (to use two conveniently vague phrases), the unqualified audit opinion implies that individual items in the audited accounts, and the audited accounts as a whole, are not materially mis-stated.

The auditor expresses an opinion on the financial statements; he does not express an opinion on the effectiveness or probity of the directors or of less senior management. If a true and fair view is shown, the users of accounts should be able to judge these – and other – issues. The audit process, however, involves collecting audit evidence from many sources in order to substantiate the validity of the techniques of financial measurement and financial disclosure adopted in the audited accounts. The auditor will therefore test exhaustively the validity of the views of the directors and their judgments which are the bases for accounting measurement and disclosure. In thus "challenging" the judgment of the directors, the auditor is not testing the honesty of their views, but rather is seeking to confirm the realism and relevance of these views. Responsible directors anxious to demonstrate their *bona fides* will respond positively to such audit "challenges", either by establishing to the auditor's satisfaction the validity of their original conclusions, or by modifying their original views in the light of fresh evidence – information or interpretation – put before them. The development of the modern audit process is dynamic. At its best, the audit contributes to the education (in the widest sense) of directors and of management and enhances their discharge of legal and social responsibilities. At least indirectly, the auditor monitors the director's perception of his obligations and assists him to discharge them.

In sum, the unqualified audit opinion confirming a true and fair view implies confirmation that management has discharged its responsibilities towards shareholders to exercise control over business resources and to make full and frank disclosure of the financial consequences of its actions and decisions, consistent with constraints defined by law and other regulatory agencies.

PART II

5 Audit Authority and Independence

Introduction

The objective of audit is to add credibility to financial statements by the expression of an independent and professionally expert opinion which confirms that the directors have discharged their obligations to prepare accounts which present a true and fair view of the results and resources of the business. To ensure credibility and lack of bias in the accounts, however, certain fundamental characteristics are essential to the discharge of the audit function. These include the inter-dependent characteristics of Authority and Independence.

With extremely limited exceptions, only those individuals who hold practising certificates from one of the four statutorily specified professional accountancy societies* are qualified by law[1] to act as auditors in Britain. The State identifies legislatively those who are qualified to act as auditors, and to that extent therefore the auditor exercises authority derived ultimately from the State. The individual professional societies, which regulate the affairs of their members, prescribe further conditions beyond the basic requirements for membership for the holding of a "practising certificate". The auditor, therefore, derives professional authority from membership of his accountancy Institute or Association and, from these further conditions for holding a practising certificate. The disciplinary sanctions available to an Institute or Association over an auditor are thus very potent because withdrawal of his practising certificate would deprive him of the right to act as auditor as effectively as would expulsion from membership.

*The Institute of Chartered Accountants in England and Wales
The Institute of Chartered Accountants of Scotland
The Institute of Chartered Accountants in Ireland
The Association of Certified Accountants.

[1] Companies Act 1976, S. 13(1).

The four legislatively specified societies are all "Chartered"; this means that their constitutions are regulated by Royal Charters, the terms of which are determined by the Crown in Privy Council. The disciplinary powers of the individual bodies are, of course, derived from their constitutions, which means in effect that they are "self-regulating" to the extent to which the State – through the Privy Council – permits them to be. Thus it can be demonstrated that the authority of the auditor is, by another route, ultimately derived from the State.

Auditors now commonly practise in firms constituted as partnerships which have unlimited liability at law and within which individual partners usually have personally unlimited liability. (There are, of course, many sole practitioners practising in their own name or in the name of a firm of which they are the sole proprietor. They equally have unlimited liability at law). There are also cases where an audit appointment is held in the personal name of a partner of a practice firm, either in a genuinely personal capacity or as named representative of his firm. When the audit appointment is held in the firm's name, the firm will designate one or more individual partners as "partner(s) in charge of the assignment" for operational practicality. Such an audit practitioner thus acts for all his partners and represents them; as an individual he really acts in a "corporate" way for the whole partnership.

Authority

Authority and social status are closely inter-dependent. Professional authority may be associated initially with evidence of educational attainment and with the display of technical skills. In Britain, various distinguishable professions have long-established traditions of separate self-regulation of membership entrance qualifications and of disciplinary powers over members. A professional organisation, therefore, can be seen as a mechanism for ensuring that those who seek to practise particular skills undertake appropriate education and training and that practitioners maintain their educational and practical levels of competence. Membership of any profession, therefore, bestows a degree of social status and thereby adds to the authority of the practitioner. To audit company accounts requires educational and technical attainments related to skills of accounting (financial measurement and reporting) and to skills of auditing.

Thus, the professional accountancy societies are of great importance in establishing and maintaining the authority of those who act as auditors. The major concerns of the accountancy societies in this regard focus on:

Education, Training and Examination for qualification; and, thereafter,

Maintenance of Professional Standards and Discipline.

The accountancy societies in Britain have to pay regard to external social influences on both these aspects if they are to maintain the authority of their members as auditors.

Authority obviously embraces the validation of expertise – without the appropriate expertise the would-be auditor cannot add credibility. Domestically within the UK other social influences stimulate the development and formalisation of continuing professional education beyond initial qualification. Harmonisation of European laws prompts consideration of the extent to which British traditions of professional education and training coincide with views elsewhere in the EEC. The proposed Fifth and Eighth EEC Directives, which are to do with educational and institutional qualifications for appointment as auditor, are therefore of current interest.

Response by the professional accountancy societies to public uncertainty about the second area of professional concern – Professional Standards and Discipline – can be seen in the exploration of issues involved in formulating Auditing Standards. The proposals for modifying and strengthening disciplinary procedures and the continuing debate about the right to "self-regulation" also indicate an awareness within the accountancy profession of concerns and pressures from outside.

Independence

Independence and Authority are both inter-related and inter-dependent; just as expertise is needed to add credibility, so is independence. If the auditor is to add credibility to the report of management, he must be independent of management – and be seen to be. If he is to confirm the absence of bias in the figures and in the financial statements, he should not be associated directly with any particular interest group. Independence is ultimately a state of mind, a matter of ethics, morality and personal philosophy. Certain basic precepts have, however, been discerned. Legal requirements define an absolute minimum of independence in the relationships between auditors and directors – an auditor cannot be a director of the company or a business partner or employee of a director.[2]

[2] Companies Act 1948, S. 161(2).

Obviously close association with management is inconsistent with the *demonstration* of the degree of independence needed to act as auditor. In the main, a pragmatic approach to finding practical evidence of independence has focused attention on avoiding conflict of interest with other obligations in the discharge of the audit function. Absence of conflict of interest, of course, does not necessarily, or of itself, assure the presence of independence.

The work of carrying out an audit demands co-operation between management and auditor. It is management who provide or control most of the information needed as audit evidence. The auditor's investigation provides him with access to privileged information. Audit firms therefore developed internal regulations intended to demonstrate that auditors would not and could not benefit personally from information obtained in the course of their work as independent auditors. These regulations include prohibition of shareholdings in client companies either by partners or their families. (A difficult and still not totally resolved problem concerns trustee shareholdings, where the auditor has no direct interest in the shares but may be subject to potential conflicts of responsibility towards the company – or at least its shareholders to whom he reports – and towards the beneficiaries of the trust of which he is a trustee. For this reason most audit firms proscribe "substantial" trustee shareholdings and others decline to allow partners to act as trustee at all).

These principles have recently been developed and adopted by the various professional societies. All auditors are now governed by "Codes of Conduct" or "Ethical Guidelines" intended to assist them in achieving and in demonstrating independence. It is an interesting paradox that, when the audit function was evolving in limited companies over one hundred years ago, the early "auditors" *were* shareholders; recognising limitations to their technical expertise such shareholder-auditors sought advice and help from practising *accountants* who gradually took over the total audit function. Auditors have thus moved from requiring a shareholding in the company being audited as a qualification for appointment to being required to demonstrate no such shareholding in order to be so qualified!

Some commentators worry about the fact that, although the audit appointment is formally made by the shareholders, in the vast majority of practical situations the Board of Directors initiates proposals for the appointment. The Board is also usually given powers, delegated from the shareholders, to negotiate audit fees. Individual firms and the professional accountancy societies are developing codes of practice in this regard also to display evidence of independence: for example, it is suggested in recent ethical guidelines that "recurrent fees" from any one client company should not exceed 15% of the total fee income of the auditor.

A final "problem area", still unresolved, is the provision by the auditor of non-audit advisory services. To some observers it appears that such provision may interfere with the appearance of independence in one or both of two ways: either by intensifying the financial dependency of the auditor on the management of the client company or by imposing on him an obligation to audit financial reports reflecting the results of management decisions influenced by his advice. A common practical illustration of this problem is the "small" company where the practising accountant, acting as the agent of management, *prepares* the financial statements which he then has to *audit* independently. Observation of this particular problem fuels the debate about relieving small companies of an audit (not a reporting) requirement. Other concerns focus on the provision of Management Consultancy Services, where it is sometimes thought that an auditor's independence is compromised because accounts showing a true and fair view may not coincide with the perceived or hoped for benefits of adopting the consultancy advice. The "ethical guidelines" at present deal with the concern of extreme financial dependency within the terms of the fee limit (15%) indicated above. The concern about managerial influence or "agency" is at present dealt with by emphasising the extreme care needed to ensure segregation and distinction of management support functions from the audit function.

In common with all professional people, the auditor is ultimately the custodian of his own conscience. He lives by his reputation; his reputation is built on the observation by his peers, his clients, and others, of his professional conduct and of his technical competence. He will assiduously strive to achieve the highest possible standard in both. By maintaining his integrity and his independence he will reinforce his authority. By upholding and enhancing his authority he will reinforce his independence. Thus he will be able to add credibility to accounts which attain a true and fair view as validated by his audit opinion. If the auditor is to ensure the relevance of the audit function and to maintain the exercise of this socially-useful activity, he must be ever-jealous of preserving his authority and his independence.

6 *Audit Evidence*

Introduction

Audit evidence tends inevitably to be persuasive rather than conclusive. Statute law, case law, and the activities of private sector agencies and organisations (including the Stock Exchange, professional societies, and representative industrial groupings) all combine in imposing on the directors the primary responsibilities of safeguarding resources and of using them effectively. The directors and the management are responsible, among many other matters, for eliminating as far as possible the existence of fraud or error. The directors have a primary responsibility to make a "true and fair" accounting of their actions. The objective of the audit function is to lend credibility to the company's accounts. The auditor is not an investigator searching for evidence of the existence of error or fraud. The auditor therefore approaches his task on the basis of a presumption that the directors (and the management) have done everything reasonably possible to discharge their primary responsibilities.

Although entitled to assume that the directors and management have acted diligently, the auditor is not entitled to ignore the possibility that his assumption is invalid. The auditor is entitled to assume the absence of significant error or fraud, but not to ignore indications of their existence. When such indications exist he must extend his investigations in an attempt to confirm either the existence or the absence of the suspected error or fraud. The auditor does not challenge the decisions of the board (other than those which relate to financial measurement and disclosure) but he ensures that the results of board decisions are properly quantified and disclosed. He should investigate unauthorised or uncontrolled use of company resources. The auditor must not ignore the possibility of the existence of error or fraud, nor must he avoid sensitive areas simply because of an initial assumption that the directors have successfully discharged their responsibilities. The auditor's primary objective is not simply to confirm that directors have successfully met a limited aspect of their overall responsibilities, but to confirm that the accounts as a whole disclose a true and fair view of the directors' activities and decisions.

It cannot be too strongly emphasised that it is the responsibility of the directors to prepare and present accounts which show a true and fair view of the state of affairs and results of the company. In achieving this objective they have to select and implement appropriate systems of financial measurement and financial reporting; they have to ensure that proper accounting records are maintained so that financial information is available for controlling resources and for informing decisions about the use and allocation of resources. So that his professional opinion can be based on a proper evaluation of whether or not the accounts show a true and fair view, the auditor seeks evidence about the directors' effective discharge of their responsibilities.

Criteria for the Audit Opinion

To the extent to which the audit opinion confirms compliance with statutorily-defined detailed disclosure requirements, the specification of these provides objectively determinable criteria of compliance. The specific requirements relate to reasonably easily observable events and therefore the audit opinion about detailed compliance can be more closely based on objective factual criteria than can the more subjective opinion about the overall true and fair view. (Of course, there may be difficulties in confirming the validity of the *measurement* of the items disclosed).

For many years the accountancy profession has been trying to assist both those who have to prepare and those who have to audit accounts by issuing guidance statements and recommendations on various technical aspects of financial measurement and disclosure. Since the beginning of the 1970s the main mechanism for such efforts with regard to accounting has been the promulgation of Statements of Standard Accounting Practice ("SSAPs"). These were originally explained as being intended to reduce the range and variety of accounting practices used in measuring or disclosing transactions or events. Some SSAPs, certainly, appear to attempt the provision of objective criteria of financial disclosure by specifying "norms" compared to which compliance could be measured in terms of fact. These particular SSAPs are thus similar to the statutory disclosure requirements. Perhaps the successes to date of the standard-setting programme have been to do with matters of disclosure rather than of measurement.

The SSAPs which appear to have caused greatest difficulty to preparers, to auditors, and to users of accounts are those which seem to limit the proper exercise of professional judgment in the inevitably complex aspects of financial measurement. Precisely because the accounting treatment of complex issues must have regard to all the particular circumstances of the transactions or events, any attempts to define universally applicable criteria for attaining a true and fair view will create rather than solve problems. This dilemma is evident in some of the more recent SSAPs, where more than one alternative has been proposed as the "standard" or "norm". Such a choice emphasises the need for judgment in deciding which "standard method" to adopt. It has to be noted in passing that by no means all the difficult issues of accounting are yet dealt with by SSAPs.

Since the objective of the accounting standards programme is to assist the process of accounting, it is expected that compliance with SSAPs will be consistent with the presentation of a "true and fair view". However, compliance with SSAPs is not of itself sufficient to result in accounts which show a true and fair view – any more than is compliance with the legally-defined disclosure requirements. Indeed, the accountancy profession recognises that there may be circumstances, albeit unusual, where the presentation of a true and fair view demands departure from the prescriptions of one or more SSAPs. The unqualified audit opinion, therefore, confirming that the accounts do show a true and fair view has to be based on consideration of evidence about the appropriateness of following SSAPs and not simply about confirmation of compliance.

Accounting Standards have been followed more recently by the initial specification of Auditing Standards (See Section 3C). The intention of Auditing Standards is apparently to provide criteria by which the auditor can assess the relevance and significance of the audit work on which he bases his audit opinion. Auditing Standards would, it is thought, will also provide users of audited accounts with a valuable indication of the procedures by which it is expected that the auditor will in normal circumstances arrive at his opinion. There are obvious dangers that Auditing Standards will be perceived as being either little more than codification of existing common practice or, at the other extreme, inflexible specification of the prescribed ingredients of an audit.

The auditing profession as a whole will continue to be the final arbiter of professional concepts of appropriate criteria for the audit opinion. Such professionally based concepts must interpret and respond to the wishes and views of other interest groups and of society at large. Although Auditing

Standards may serve to express some of the concepts of audit criteria, the forum where the relevance and adequacy of audit criteria will be tested ultimately will continue to be the Law Courts. In that forum legal issues as to what is "reasonable" will be determined with the help of expert evidence about professional expectations. Inherent in the audit process is the problem that legal issues only arise in association with subsequent *prima facie* indications that the audited accounts did not show a true and fair view. That is, the issue comes before the Courts only when there is already a *prima facie* indication that the criteria on which the opinion was based were *not* appropriate!

The brief discussion earlier, in Section 2, about the true and fair view made clear the imprecise and subjective nature of that concept. Obviously, discussion of the audit evidence which is needed as a basis for an opinion about a true and fair view must also be imprecise and emphasise its subjective nature. Because "true and fair" has connotations of "lack of bias", "adequate", "relevant", etc, audit evidence will relate to confirming that the accounts do exhibit these qualities. Although he is not their agent in a "conflict" with the directors, the auditor will be mindful of his appointment by shareholders, of the fact that he reports to them and of his objective of lending credibility to accounts prepared primarily for shareholders. In considering his audit opinion, therefore, he will, to some extent at least, stand in the shoes of the shareholder and consider whether or not a reasonably informed shareholder would reasonably interpret the audited accounts in such a way as to conclude that the accounts actually disclosed the state of affairs which the auditor, based on his detailed examination and evidence, believes to exist.

The true and fair view is closely associated with the idea of materiality, and audit evidence also has to be assembled and assessed in the context of materiality. This concept, it has been shown, has dimensions of quality (nature of the item) and of quantity (size of the item). Audit evidence, therefore, must also recognise these different dimensions. It should be noted that, since the audit opinion is based on previously prepared financial statements, audit evidence is more readily accessible about items which have been included in the accounts than about those which do not appear. It is inherently easier to identify items which have been incorrectly included than it is to speculate about those incorrectly omitted. In the context of materiality there is an upper limit to the amount of error of overstatement in the accounts (the financial value attributed the item wrongly included), but there is in principle no upper limit to the amount of understatement.

Conclusion

"Judgment permeates the auditor's work. . . ."[1] An attempt has been made here to demonstrate that the criteria by which the auditor finally assesses the success (or otherwise) of management in preparing accounts which show a true and fair view are themselves the result of *his* exercise of audit judgment. Audit judgment permeates the following aspects of the auditor's work:

planning the allocation of staff to tasks;

determining the existence, nature and effectiveness of "internal control";

deciding the nature of audit evidence required;

deciding the detailed selection of individual items for specific audit testing;

evaluating the results of audit tests;

evaluating audit evidence as a whole;

assessing the financial statements as a whole.

The audit objective is an opinion confirming the discharge of the directors' financial reporting obligations. The preparation of financial statements demands the exercise of judgment; absolute accuracy is unattainable and uncertainty cannot be eliminated. The audit process, designed to minimise the existence of inaccuracy and uncertainty in accounts, also involves the exercise of further judgment. Audited accounts are inevitably associated with risks that:

the accounts contain undetected error; and/or

the audit opinion is based on erroneous interpretation of the evidence.

The audit function demands the highest degree of professional skill directed to minimising the risk that either of these errors remains after the audit examination.

[1] IFAC. International Auditing Guideline No. 1. "Objective and Scope of the Audit of Financial Statements". (1980).

7 The Audit Process

A brief review of the practical process of auditing is needed to explain *how* the audit function is discharged. Such a review will also help towards an understanding of the meaning of the audit report. The following discussion, however, can only provide an overview of the outlines of the audit process; it is not a substitute for other, fuller, texts which describe and justify detailed aspects of audit practice.

Scope of Audit Examination

The view of audit responsibility as defined statutorily excludes any possibility of imposing restrictions on the scope of the audit examination. It is for the auditor himself to decide the scope of examination which is appropriate as a basis for the exercise of his professional audit judgment. The auditor bears sole responsibility for any deficiencies in audit performance which might be due to restriction of the scope of examination (or to lack of prosecution in resolving audit uncertainties).

The legislation which requires, and defines the nature of, the audit opinion also arms the auditor with rights of access to evidence. He is entitled to have access at all times to the books, records and vouchers of the company.[1] Further, he has legally enforceable powers to require from the "officers of the company" (that is the directors and the management) such information and explanations as he, the auditor, thinks necessary for the performance of his duties. In 1976 it became a criminal offence for any director or officer knowingly or recklessly to mislead the auditor in the course of his pursuit of information and explanations.[2]

[1] Companies Act 1967, S. 14(5).
[2] Companies Act 1976, S. 19.

Although the audit opinion relates explicitly to the formal accounts, the audit examination extends to all the company's records from which such financial statements are derived. It embraces the documents and vouchers which directly validate the accuracy of individual entries in the accounting records. Since the accounting records constitute a financial model of the business operations of the company the audit examination may well extend to evidence which is itself not expressed in financial terms. The initial professional statements of Auditing Standards include "The Auditor's Operational Standard" which summarises the position as follows:–

> "*Planning, Controlling and Recording*
> The auditor should adequately plan, control and record his work.
>
> *Accounting Systems*
> The auditor should ascertain the enterprise's system of recording and processing transactions and assess its adequacy as a basis for the preparation of financial statements.
>
> *Audit Evidence*
> The auditor should obtain relevant and reliable audit evidence sufficient to enable him to draw reasonable conclusions therefrom.
>
> *Internal Control*
> If the auditor wishes to place reliance on any internal controls, he should ascertain and evaluate those controls and perform compliance tests on their operation.
>
> *Review of Financial Statements*
> The auditor should carry out such a review of the financial statements as is sufficient in conjunction with the conclusions drawn from the other audit evidence obtained, to give him a reasonable basis for his opinion on the financial statements".

In attaining the audit objective the auditor has to consider whether or not proper accounting records have been maintained by the company; a professional obligation explicitly reinforced by statute law.[3] Whether "accounting records" are adequate (or "proper") has to be judged by considering the extent to which management has secured compliance with statutorily-defined requirements.[4] The key requirements are that "the accounting records shall be sufficient to show and explain the company's transactions"

[3] Companies Act 1967, S. 14(4).
[4] Companies Act 1976, S. 12.

and that "the accounting records shall be such as to disclose with reasonable accuracy at any time the financial position of the company at that time and enable the directors to ensure that any balance sheet or profit and loss account prepared by them ... complies with the requirements [to show a true and fair view] ".

The recently published Auditing Guideline on Internal Controls which supplements The Auditor's Operational Standard quoted above reiterates management responsibility for internal control as follows:–

> "It is the responsibility of management to decide the extent of the internal control system which is appropriate to the enterprise".

The Guideline also emphasises that the nature and extent of controls will depend upon many factors such as nature, size and volume of transactions and the size, location and managerial organisation of the enterprise.

The present general understanding that the audit examination includes and is, to some extent at least, based on review and appraisal of the company's control systems is also confirmed by the Guideline as follows:–

> ". . . . the auditor will have to decide the extent to which he wishes to place reliance on the internal controls of the enterprise".

> "The auditor's objective in evaluating and testing internal controls is to determine the degree of reliance which he places on the information contained in the accounting records. If he obtains reasonable answers by means of compliance tests that the internal controls are effective . . . . he may limit the extent of his substantive testing".

Substantive testing includes procedures such as analytical review of accounts and of financial statements and also tests of individual transactions and balances.

Work of detailed audit examination is usually based on a restricted number of selected items which are representative of similar transactions, or types of transactions, or items. Important audit decisions have to be taken about the emphasis of audit testing – both in determining the nature of transactions or items to be tested and in selecting the individual transactions or items for detailed testing. Audit testing provides only a part of the total evidence but is specifically referred to here because an understanding of the audit process demands a realisation that not all transactions or items are specifically confirmed by direct evidence. Given the probabilities of error inherent in financial measurement and reporting, even total examination could not provide complete assurance of accuracy.

Audit Techniques

Various audit techniques which tend to concentrate on methods of assembling recorded audit evidence have been evolved, including those directed towards:–

– recording systems of control;

– evaluating the effectiveness of control;

– sampling for detailed testing, on bases which can be statistically evaluated and on "judgment" bases;

– statistical evaluation of detailed testing;

– computer-based systems and computer-maintained records;

– formal recording of evidence of audit work done and audit conclusions;

– obtaining "independent" confirmation from external sources;

– physical examination of tangible assets or of documents of title;

– reviewing financial statements as a whole for credibility and feasibility, *ie* "analytical review".

Different auditors will give different emphasis to the various aspects of audit evidence. Different audit techniques – or different modifications of similar techniques – have been developed by individual auditors, or, more precisely, by individual audit firms. A commonly adopted audit approach is currently the so-called "systems based audit", under which the company's control systems are examined in detail as a basis for identifying areas of relatively high audit risk. These are the areas of the accounting system associated with a high degree of risk that the financial statements submitted for audit contain undetected error or those associated with a high degree of risk that failure to detect any error in the financial statements would be considered to be a serious audit failure. The detailed audit evidence relating to individual items – that is the evidence of "substantive testing" – is then assembled on the basis of the perceived audit risk. Substantive tests include confirmation of existence and of quantification. The extent and nature of substantive testing, therefore, depends upon the decisions taken about the effectiveness of systems of internal control – hence the phrase "systems based audit".

The three main types of audit evidence contributing towards overall "audit assurance" are:–

– evaluation of the effectiveness and integrity of control and reporting systems ("systems evaluation");

– detailed examination of and confirmation of the validity of the measurement and disclosure of individual items and transactions or groups of items and transactions ("substantive testing");

– evaluation of the financial statements as a whole and review for credibility, feasibility, and consistency ("analytical review").

Each of these elements demands the exercise of audit judgment in deciding what evidence to seek and in collecting and evaluating the evidence. The total "audit assurance" is the result of audit judgment in deciding the "blend" of elements appropriate in an individual case.

Audit evidence will, of course, relate both to transactions reflected in the profit and loss account and to closing balances appearing in the balance sheet. There often tends to be an audit emphasis on the verification of balance sheet items. Frequently a higher proportion of these may be selected for detailed audit examination than is selected of the usually more numerous accounting entries reflecting revenue transactions. This emphasis is not necessarily the result of a simplistic argument along the lines of:–

> "If the entries in the opening and closing balance sheets can be validated then the intermediate profit and loss account will be validated by inference."

Audit emphasis on the balance sheet reflects the different nature of the items and, therefore, of the type of audit evidence available. Balance sheet figures reflect the existence of assets and liabilities and relate to incomplete transactions. It is often possible to obtain direct evidence of the existence of balance sheet items – for example, physical assets, such as stock or machinery, can be and usually are physically examined to provide audit evidence of existence, condition and location. This illustrative discussion, however, provides an incomplete picture. Some auditors design their audit tests so that revenue transactions are subjected to the same degree of detailed scrutiny as are balance sheet entries, particularly where statistical sampling plans are applied across all the accounting records and not just related to balance sheet items.

As has been made clear in earlier discussion, the audit opinion relates to the formal accounts as a whole. Audit evidence which was restricted to individual entries in the accounting records would be an insufficient basis for an audit opinion on the overall financial reporting of the company. In addition to examining individual trees the wood as a whole has to be surveyed. The accounts as a whole are subjected to an overall review for reliability, feasibility, credibility and consistency – "do they make sense?". The auditor relates the financial statements as a whole to all that he knows of the accounting records, of the company, of its industry and of the economic environment. The unqualified audit opinion about the true and fair view confirms that the accounts are a reasonable representation of reality.

8 *The Importance of the Audit Report*

This paper has sought to demonstrate that audited accounts are an important element in the discharge by management (led by the directors) of reporting obligations to shareholders. The audit opinion provides independent confirmation that management has maintained proper records of transactions and has made true and fair disclosure of the consequences of these transactions. The law provides that the auditor be formally appointed by shareholders and that he reports to them. The primary responsibility for ensuring that the accounts do show a true and fair view is borne by the directors (also appointed by the shareholders) who have a statutorily-defined duty to prepare and submit such accounts to the shareholders. The auditor's responsibility is for the *opinion* he expresses in the audit report addressed to and relating to accounts prepared for shareholders. Audited accounts are used extensively by shareholders and also by others.

Because of the nature of the processes of accounting and of auditing, audited accounts cannot possess any quality of universality. What is seen to be appropriate for a true and fair view from the point of perception of shareholders does not necessarily provide the appropriate financial measurement or disclosure for others with interests in the corporate enterprise. However, the existence of the audit opinion on accounts prepared for shareholders does enable other users to place greater reliance on these accounts than would be possible without audit. Although the auditor owes no statutory duty to report to other users of the audited accounts, he owes them the same professional duty with regard to his report as he owes to those to whom the report is addressed. The auditor has to be aware of the fact that the existence of the audit report has significance for them; he acquires additional, non-statutory responsibilities towards those who take decisions based on the existence of his audit opinion. Thus it is that the nature and extent of the auditor's responsibilities have been progressively and very considerably extended. Those to whom the audit report is explicitly addressed are only one of many groups who place reliance on the audit opinion. Perhaps the greatest fault an auditor can betray, perhaps his only fault, is to be seen to have made a mistake; his authority and status seem to require that his opinion is seen to be always justifiable.

The use of accounts by the taxation authorities provides an obvious example of the benefit to a non-shareholder of the audit opinion. Fiscal rules for calculating profits assessable to tax do not necessarily coincide with bases of measurement and disclosure considered appropriate for financial reporting to shareholders. (UK practice in this regard contrasts with practice in some other countries which require company accounts to follow fiscal principles). The starting point for computing assessable corporate profits, however, is the figure of profit disclosed in the audited accounts; because the audit report addressed to shareholders minimises the extent and nature of detailed examination which the Inland Revenue might otherwise think necessary, audited figures can be relied on as a basis for computing tax liabilities. (It may be noted in passing that in some other countries where the independent audit function is less well developed than in the UK there is a separate "tax audit" by the tax authorities distinct from the audit for shareholders).

Banks and financial institutions place reliance on audited accounts, although they also frequently ask for additional information beyond that disclosed in the audited accounts. These specific requests demonstrate that accounts prepared for shareholders are not necessarily universally complete for the purposes of other users. Such institutions often require independent verification of, or opinion on, the supplementary information and in such cases usually ask the company's auditor to provide the specific validation or opinion. As for the Inland Revenue, audited accounts also provide a useful basis of validated financial information for these institutions, and the audited accounts are expanded by only limited detailed re-examination or supplementation.

The Stock Exchange relies upon the existence of audited accounts as part of its mechanism for ensuring that the securities and capital markets are informed about the financial affairs and status of companies whose shares are listed. Audited accounts specifically giving a true and fair view to shareholders are obviously of direct relevance to the information needs of those who use the facilities of the Stock Exchange. Audited accounts also provide important validation of the financial impact on the company of events and transactions of which the investor may be aware but able only to estimate the financial significance for the company. Audited accounts provide for investors at least subsequent confirmation of the validity (or otherwise) of investor expectations of company performance.

Financial reporting to employees is a topic of current interest. Much remains to be done in defining the information needs of employees and in contrasting these with the conventional accounts disclosing a true and fair view to shareholders. It is already clear that employee organisations, including Trade Unions, have access to and make use of information reported to shareholders. Trade Unions and other employee organisations, however, have not yet clarified their attitudes to the need for validation of other financial information reported to employees. Employees and their representatives seem to have incomplete understanding of the audit function and of its relevance to their information needs. The concept of audit independence seems not to be widely appreciated and the auditor appears (wrongly) to be thought of as being part of the management. Validation is not only relevant in the context of annual reports for the total entity but arguably more so in the context of the specific financial information produced for individual locations or departments. Validation certainly seems appropriate in the context of disclosure of financial information for collective bargaining, or in compliance with other statutory disclosure requirements of UK employment legislation.

Audited accounts are used and referred to by many interests which seek information about the allocation of company resources and results among the groups who contribute to the creation of wealth – shareholders, lenders, employees, suppliers, customers and the community at large. Audited accounts are extremely important to the individual and to the community and are used for many purposes, including the following:

– to judge managerial effectiveness;

– to calculate tax liabilities;

– as a basis for providing and maintaining credit facilities;

– for investment decisions, including the purchase and sale of shares;

– in assisting the determination of the legality of certain transactions – *eg* borrowing limits, dividend payments, etc;

– in determining contractual obligations – *eg* commissions or profit-sharing arrangements;

– to provide information about the financial stability of the company to those trading with it, including customers and suppliers;

– referred to in wage negotiation;

– in assisting the design and implementation of national economic and social policies.

It is hoped that the significance of the audit report will be better understood following this review of the nature of the audit function, its objectives and some characteristics of the audit process. Perhaps it has become clearer to the reader what the audit report means and, maybe even more importantly, what it does not mean!

9 *Some Unresolved Problems*

Introduction

When a society's structures and goals are changing rapidly, a socially-responsive activity such as financial reporting will inevitably generate problems. Some which seem to affect the auditor and which have been identified and become important recently and in which influences of social change can be expected to be important in the near future, are referred to briefly in the following paragraphs.

Insider Dealing

We have asserted earlier that the auditor is not the custodian of the conscience of management. We have, however, also noted, in Section 4, that there is considerable public uncertainty about the role of the auditor when the actions of directors conflict with their "trusteeship" responsibilities towards shareholders. The debate and discussion about "insider dealing" by directors and transactions by them in the shares of their company exemplify these concerns and uncertainties. The developing doctrine of accountability appears to be leading to a proposition that anybody involved in the direction or management of a company should be seen to be beyond suspicion of obtaining any improper personal benefit derived from his office. Such benefit might be derived from his control of the resources of the company or from information he obtains while acting as agent of the shareholders. It is also clear that any personal benefit properly received – for example, salary, etc – should be carefully quantified and disclosed. The "crisis of authority" impinges on directors to the extent that they have to be able to demonstrate that they are not abusing the authority vested in them by shareholders.

Questionable Payments

What are called "illegal and corrupt practices" have also become an area of public concern and discussion. Reports of enquiries undertaken in recent years by inspectors appointed by the Department of Trade have provided the bases for some public discussion about the conduct of company directors. A number of the reports highlight circumstances indicating the existence of a failure of accountability. Some recent developments in the United States of America have also stimulated discussion of the relevance of USA experiences for United Kingdom circumstances. The problem of "trans-national influences" is most pronounced in the context of the multinational corporation with operations in a number of countries.

There are two rather different perspectives. The first dimension might be seen to be commercial transactions and relationships which contravene the law or code of morality in the country within which the headquarters of the corporation are based and where its ultimate reporting takes place, but which do not contravene the social expectations or the law of the particular country in which the transaction occurs. An example could be the bribery of officials in overseas territories in order to expedite customs clearance or to facilitate normal commercial transactions. The American approach to this aspect of the problem is to ensure that arrangements and procedures exist which enable the ultimate authority (the board of directors) of the reporting entity to be informed about what is going on in all parts of the world where operations under their control occur. It leaves to members of the parent Board the responsibility for informing themselves of what is going on, and for satisfying themselves that what has occurred is, in general terms, "acceptable". Developments in the USA are leading to a position where the auditor may well have specific responsibility for ensuring, and reporting his opinion, that systems of managerial control do in fact exist which enable the ultimate authority to be informed and to take decisions about what occurs in overseas territories. What is not yet resolved is how the results or the consequences of these transactions should be reported.

A second dimension comprises those transactions which are not seen as "objectionable" from the perceptions of the society within which the ultimate controlling parent is reporting but which are objectionable from the view-point of the local community within which an individual entity is operating and undertaking these transactions. An example might be found in a multinational based in a country which does not share Western European views of business morality but has units operating in Western Europe. Both the United Nations and the Organisation for Economic Co-operation and

Development, as multinational agencies, are exploring this problem and are anxious to evolve appropriate "codes of conduct" for multinationals in an attempt to harmonise their relationships with local host communities and with their base communities of origin and ultimate control.

International Accounting Standards

Similar attempts to achieve "harmonisation" of financial reporting are also being developed by international governmental agencies and international groupings of accountancy organisations. These will presumably lead ultimately to attempts to harmonise techniques of financial measurement. Attempts are also being made to move towards some harmonisation of institutional perceptions of audit objectives. This, in turn, is likely to have implications for the evolution of "harmonised" audit techniques. Such progress towards international perceptions of financial reporting must be viewed against a background of the locally responsive nature of accountancy and auditing developments.

Management Audit

Discussion continues about the possibility of some form of "management audit". It appears that already in some Scandinavian countries auditors report to shareholders as to the effectiveness with which management has conducted the affairs of the company during the reporting period. The question of "efficiency" or of "value for money" audit is a matter of concern in the United Kingdom, more particularly in public sector undertakings where normal criteria of profit are either not available or are not considered appropriate as an indicator of managerial effectiveness. In public sector enterprises there are no shareholders as such to decide about the efficiency with which a management has operated resources under its control, and the direct intervention of the auditor seems to be considered an appropriate means of testing whether or not social objectives have been achieved. The development of appropriate relationships between internal audit and external audit is also seen as an aspect of these particular problems. Development or extension of management audit will prompt review of the range of technical skills needed by an auditor.

Audit Committees

It is thought by some that relationships between the auditor and the board would be better regulated if the board were to establish an audit committee. Typically an audit committee would consist of a small number of directors, predominantly non-executive. Audit Committees are also seen by some as being helpful in defining the responsibilities of the board as a whole and of non-executive directors within the board, particularly with regard to the annual accounts. The idea of audit committees is effectively an importation from North America and its development in the UK is proceeding cautiously.

Peer Review – Quis Custodiet?

Another North American development is the institution there of "peer reviews". This may be referred to in simple terms as an audit of the auditors. Under a peer review system as developed so far in the USA the procedures within an audit firm for organising and supervising its planning and execution of audit work is subject to review and report by another audit firm (at present usually confidentially). It is appropriate that there should be careful and analytical thought about the relevance to the United Kingdom context of such a development, however appropriate it may be in the distinguishable North American circumstances. The political, social and legal structures of the USA are significantly different from those of the UK. The organisation of the capital markets and the structure and organisation of many corporations are different and certainly the structure, organisation, objectives and role of the public accounting firms are quite different in North America from those in the United Kingdom. The perceptions of the audit function differ accordingly, as do arrangements for assuring its proper discharge.

Small Company Audits

The desirability of relieving so-called "small" companies in the UK from an audit requirement in certain circumstances is currently under discussion. This development results in part from the work of APC, in part from the approval by the EEC of the 4th Directive on Company Law which, among other matters, highlights the possibility of UK legislation exempting "small" companies from audit. The discussion also reflects improved understanding in professional and general circles of the significance of the audit function. The quality of audit evidence available in such companies inevitably differs from that available in the large corporation with segregation of responsibilities and scope for carefully designed control procedures. It is now better realised that reporting objectives and standards of accounting records and control procedures in "small" companies are such that in many cases there will be insufficient independent audit evidence on which to base an unqualified audit opinion. The issues, however, have not yet been fully defined and, to some extent at least, are still confused with different issues, including the possibility of "simplifying" the financial disclosure of "small" and "medium-sized" companies. It certainly seems likely that the audit report on the accounts of "small" companies will differ in many cases from the "standard" unqualified report discussed in this monograph.

Inflation-adjusted Accounts

Finally, brief reference should be made again to a problem touched on earlier. That is the question of the credibility of accounts based on historical cost measurements and the need to develop methods of financial reporting which reflect the impact of changing price levels. SSAP 16 (published in March 1980) summarises the objectives of CCA accounts as being "to provide *more useful* information than that available from historical cost accounts *alone* for the guidance of the management of the business, the shareholders and others. . . ." (para 5 of Explanatory Note, emphasis added). As referred to in earlier discussion (in Section 3A), the application of SSAP 16 is restricted to "large entities" and not all companies will yet be required to prepare CCA accounts. Although the terms of the Standard explicitly admit of the possibility that CCA accounts may be produced as the main or only accounts, it is also clearly stated that "the great majority of companies" will probably decide to retain historical cost accounts as the main accounts (para 28 of Explanatory Note).

The time may come when either both historical-cost and CCA accounts are regarded as essential to the presentation of a true and fair view, or CCA accounts alone may come to be regarded as the basic "true and fair" accounts (with historical cost information, if provided at all, given only in supplementary statements). The terms of audit report will have to change accordingly.

Following the development during the early 1970s of ideas for reflecting the impact of changing price levels by providing additional Current Purchasing Power ("CPP") accounts, an audit report was evolved which confirmed the "fair restatement" (of historical cost accounts) in the CPP accounts. Subsequent developments led to supplementary Current Cost Accounting ("CCA") financial statements. Surveys of financial reporting by major companies during 1978 and 1979 indicated that about one-half of these supplementary CCA accounts were reported on by auditors. The audit reports in these cases varied considerably. Some offered an opinion that the supplementary statements were "true and fair" according to the CCA convention, others that they were "properly prepared" or were "in compliance" with the relevant accountancy proposals. At least some of the initial problems of auditing CCA statements, of course, derived from their status as *supplementary* (to the historical cost accounts) and from difficulties in perceiving the objective of the accounts themselves. SSAP 16 now uses the word "*additional*" in relation to CCA accounts which has subtly different implications from the former description of "supplementary". At the time of writing, APC has recently indicated its intention to prepare and distribute a discussion document outlining its views on an appropriate audit response to the CCA statements which will be required under SSAP 16. Views expressed on this discussion document will influence the formulation of the institutional response to the audit issues raised by recent accounting developments.

The audit response so far to proposals for providing financial information on the basis of the CCA system has tended to confuse the perceptions of audit objectives. Questions still unresolved include:

– should CCA accounts be reported on by the auditor?;

– if so, in what terms should the report be phrased?;

– when audited CCA accounts are provided should there continue to be an audit report on the historical cost accounts?

Determination of an audit response can, of course, only follow the evolution of a generally accepted accounting process. That preliminary step is still to be accomplished and it would be a mistake to see SSAP 16 as other than marking the end of one stage towards the ultimate attainment of that objective. Therefore the audit response is obviously not yet clear.

Conclusion

These few brief paragraphs have served to highlight some of the areas in which current auditing developments can be observed. Such developments can be expected to provide issues for active debate. It should be clear that as concepts of accountability change so the perceptions of audit objectives and audit responsibilities will change. It is essential that users, preparers and auditors of accounts continue to co-operate in discerning the extent to which social expectations change and thus help each other towards the proper discharge of their individual responsibilities.

Appendix I

Auditing Standard - The Audit Report

(issued April 1980)

The Audit Report

This Auditing Standard should be read in conjunction with the Explanatory Foreword to Auditing Standards and Guidelines including the Glossary of Terms. Qualifications in audit reports are dealt with in the Auditing Standard "Qualifications in Audit Reports". Examples of audit reports which will conform to this Standard are given in the Auditing Guideline "Audit Report Examples". The considerations which arise when reporting on financial statements not required to give a true and fair view will be dealt with subsequently.

PART 1: STATEMENT OF AUDITING STANDARD

1. This Auditing Standard applies to all reports in which the auditor expresses an opinion on financial statements intended to give a true and fair view of the state of affairs, profit or loss and, where applicable, source and application of funds. The Standard is not intended to override the statutory exemptions granted in respect of certain types of enterprise but is intended to apply to the audit reports relating to such enterprises in other respects.

2. The audit report should identify those to whom it is addressed and the financial statements to which it relates.

3. The auditor should refer expressly in his report to the following:

(*a*) whether the financial statements have been audited in accordance with approved Auditing Standards;

(*b*) whether in the auditor's opinion the financial statements give a true and fair view of the state of affairs, profit or loss and, where applicable, source and application of funds; and

(*c*) any matters prescribed by relevant legislation or other requirements.

Effective date

4. This Auditing Standard is effective for the audit of financial statements relating to accounting periods starting on or after 1st April, 1980.

PART 2: EXPLANATORY NOTE

Compliance with Approved Auditing Standards

5. The auditor should comply with approved Auditing Standards and it is appropriate that his report should refer to this fact in arriving at his opinion. Approved Auditing Standards are defined as those Statements of Auditing Standards which are approved for issue by the Councils of the accountancy bodies listed in the Explanatory Foreword and which are effective for the period covered by the financial statements on which the auditor is reporting.

True and Fair

6. The majority of audit reports are issued under the Companies Acts which normally require the use of the words "true and fair view". For the purpose of this standard, therefore, the phrase "true and fair view" has been retained. When expressing an opinion that financial statements give a true and fair view the auditor should be satisfied, *inter alia*, that:

(*a*) all relevant Statements of Standard Accounting Practice have been complied with, except in situations in which for justifiable reasons they are not strictly applicable because they are impracticable or, exceptionally, having regard to the circumstances, would be inappropriate or give a misleading view; and

(*b*) any significant accounting policies which are not the subject of Statements of Standard Accounting Practice are appropriate to the circumstances of the business.

Reference to Accounting Convention

7. The auditor should refer in his report to the particular convention used in preparing the financial statements if he considers it necessary in order to avoid misunderstanding.

Emphasis of Matter

8. As a general principle the auditor issuing an unqualified opinion should not make reference to specific aspects of the financial statements in the body of his report as such reference may be misconstrued as being a qualification. In rare circumstances, however, the reader will obtain a better understanding of the financial statements if his attention is drawn to important matters. Examples might include an unusual event, accounting policy or condition, awareness of which is fundamental to an understanding of the financial statements.

9. In order to avoid giving the impression that a qualification is intended, references which are intended as emphasis of matter should be contained in a separate paragraph and introduced with a phrase such as "We draw attention to . . ." and should not be referred to in the opinion paragraph. Emphasis of matter should not be used to rectify a lack of appropriate disclosure in the financial statements, nor should it be regarded as a substitute for a qualification.

Compliance with Relevant Legislation or other Requirements

10. The auditor should comply with any reporting requirements imposed by legislation and any other reporting requirements relevant to the financial statements. It should be noted that the Companies Acts of Great Britain, Northern Ireland and the Republic of Ireland contain different reporting requirements.

Wording of Report

11. Set out below is a form of audit report appropriate to a company incorporated in Great Britain which meets the requirements of this standard where the auditor is able to report affirmatively on all the matters contained in paragraph 3 above.

"Auditor's report to the members of

. . . .

We have audited the financial statements on pages . . . . to . . . . in accordance with approved Auditing Standards.

In our opinion the financial statements [which have been prepared under the historical cost convention as modified by the revaluation of land and buildings], give a true and fair view of the state of the company's affairs at 31st December 19 ..... and of its profit and source of application of funds for the year then ended and comply with the Companies Acts 1948 and 1967."

12. An example of an unqualified audit report appropriate to a company incorporated in Ireland is given, together with other examples of audit reports in the Auditing Guideline "Audit Report Examples" (not reproduced).

11-2-86
U097288
Van Nostrand